# The Law of Fund-Raising

# NONPROFIT LAW, FINANCE, AND MANAGEMENT SERIES

# The Law of Fund-Raising

**Second Edition
2000 Cumulative Supplement**

**BRUCE R. HOPKINS**

**John Wiley & Sons, Inc.**
New York • Chichester • Weinheim • Brisbane • Singapore • Toronto

Copyright © 2000 by John Wiley & Sons, Inc. All rights reserved.

Published simultaneously in Canada.

This publication is designed to provide accurate and
authoritative information in regard to the subject
matter covered. It is sold with the understanding that
the publisher is not engaged in rendering legal, accounting,
or other professional services. If legal advice or other
expert assistance is required, the services of a competent
professional person should be sought.

**Library of Congress Cataloging in Publication Data:**

Hopkins, Bruce R.
    The law of fund-raising / Bruce R. Hopkins.—2d ed.
      p.    cm.—(Nonprofit law, finance, and management series)
    Includes bibliographical references.
    ISBN 0-471-12534-2 (cloth : acid-free paper)
    ISBN 0-471-36129-1 (supplement)
    1. Fund raising—Law and legislation—United States.
    2. Charitable uses, trusts, and foundations—United States.
    I. Title.  II. Series.
    KF1389.5.HGG  1996
    344.73'03170681—dc20
    [347.3043170681]  95-9551

Printed in the United States of America.

10  9  8  7  6  5  4  3  2  1

# Subscriber Update Service

## BECOME A SUBSCRIBER!
### *Did you purchase this product from a bookstore?*

If you did, it's important for you to become a subscriber. John Wiley & Sons, Inc., may publish, on a periodic basis, supplements and new editions to reflect the latest changes in the subject matter that you *need to know* in order to stay competitive in this ever-changing industry. By contacting the Wiley office nearest you, you'll receive any current update at no additional charge. In addition, you'll receive future updates and revised or related volumes on a 30-day examination review.

If you purchased this product directly from John Wiley & Sons, Inc., we have already recorded your subscription for this update service.

To become a subscriber, please call **1-800-225-5945** or send your name, company name (if applicable), address, and the title of the product to:

mailing address:     **Supplement Department**
**John Wiley & Sons, Inc.**
**One Wiley Drive**
**Somerset, NJ 08875**

e-mail:          **subscriber@wiley.com**
fax:             **1-732-302-2300**
online:          **www.wiley.com**

For customers outside the United States, please contact the Wiley office nearest you:

Professional & Reference Division
John Wiley & Sons Canada, Ltd.
22 Worcester Road
Rexdale, Ontario M9W 1L1
CANADA
(416) 675-3580
Phone: 1-800-567-4797
Fax: 1-800-565-6802
canada@jwiley.com

Jacaranda Wiley Ltd.
PRT Division
P.O. Box 174
North Ryde, NSW 2113
AUSTRALIA
Phone: (02) 805-1100
Fax: (02) 805-1597
headoffice@jacwiley.com.au

John Wiley & Sons, Ltd.
Baffins Lane
Chichester
West Sussex, PO19 1UD
ENGLAND
Phone: (44) 1243 779777
Fax: (44) 1243 770638
cs-books@wiley.co.uk

John Wiley & Sons (SEA) Pte. Ltd.
37 Jalan Pemimpin
Block B #05-04
Union Industrial Building
SINGAPORE 2057
Phone: (65) 258-1157
Fax: (65) 463-4604
csd_ord@wiley.com.sg

# About the Author

**Bruce R. Hopkins** is a lawyer in Kansas City, Missouri, having practiced law in Washington, D.C., for 27 years. He specializes in the representation of nonprofit organizations. He has served as Chair of the Committee on Exempt Organizations, Section on Taxation, American Bar Association; Chair, Section on Taxation, National Association of College and University Attorneys; and President, Planned Giving Study Group of Greater Washington, D.C. He was accorded the Assistant Commissioner's (IRS) Award in 1984. He also teaches a course on nonprofit organizations at the University of Missouri-Kansas City School of Law.

Mr. Hopkins is the series editor of Wiley's Nonprofit Law, Finance, and Management Series. In addition to *The Law of Fund-Raising, Second Edition,* he is the author of *The Legal Answer Book for Nonprofit Organizations; The Second Legal Answer Book for Nonprofit Organizations; The Law of Tax-Exempt Organizations, Seventh Edition; Charity, Advocacy and the Law; The Nonprofit Law Dictionary; The Tax Law of Charitable Giving;* and *A Legal Guide to Starting and Managing a Nonprofit Organization, Second Edition;* and is co-author of *Intermediate Sanctions: Curbing Nonprofit Abuse* (with D. Benson Tesdahl); *Private Foundations: Tax Law and Compliance* (with Jody Blazek); and *The Law of Tax-Exempt Healthcare Organizations* (with Thomas K. Hyatt). He also writes *The Nonprofit Counsel,* a monthly newsletter, published by John Wiley & Sons.

Mr. Hopkins earned his J.D. and LL.M. degrees at The George Washington University and his B.A. at the University of Michigan.

# Preface

The purpose of this cumulative supplement is to summarize developments in the law of fund-raising that have transpired since publication of the main book, that is, during 1996 to 1998, and most of 1999.

Consistent with the trend over recent years, state statutory law expansion has continued apace. This includes revised (and more extensive) laws in Alabama, Colorado, Mississippi, and New Hampshire, and a new statute in Delaware. The new rules are summarized in this cumulative supplement, as additions to Chapter 3. These changes have had considerable ripple effects, which are reflected in Chapter 4, the comparative analysis chapter. In a significant development in 1998, a federal district court upheld the Charitable Solicitations Act in the state of Utah; this opinion is detailed in material added to Chapter 5, § 3.

A positive development ocurred in 1999, when a significant portion of the states agreed to a standardized registratrion form. This document, and some accompanying explanatory material, are reproduced in new Appendix J.

There is growing attention to fund-raising regulation by means of city and county ordinances. In 1997, a federal court issued an important opinion, finding two of these ordinances (those for the city and county of Los Angeles) unconstitutional for a variety of reasons. This opinion is discussed in material added to Chapter 5, § 3. By contrast, a constitutional law challenge to the Pinellas County, Florida, ordinance was not successful; the court pointedly refused to recognize the crushing burden these ordinances can—collectively—impose on charitable fund-raising. There is a discussion of these points in material added to Chapters 4, § 21; 5, § 2; and 5, § 3.

Not surprisingly, law at the federal level is also changing (and increasing) dramatically. Three developments directly affecting charitable fund-raising warrant mention. One involves the long-awaited enactment of the intermediate sanctions legislation, principally applicable to public charities. These sanctions (detailed in a separate Wiley book) introduced the concept of *excess benefit transactions,* which—along with other aspects of the intermediate sanctions law—is having a major impact of the functions of charitable organizations, including fund-raising practices and compensation. This law, which came into being in 1996 and amplified by proposed regulations issued in 1998, is discussed from a fund-raising perspective in this supplement, as part of Chapter 8, § 15A. These proposed regulations, by the way, are undergoing revision and may be expected in final form sometime in 2000.

Second, the Tax Court finally issued its holding in the *United Cancer Council* case. Finding for the government, the court illustrated how a fund-raising company can be an insider with respect to a charity and thus subject to the private inurement rules. In an astonishing development, however, this decision was reversed on appeal. These opinions are summarized in this cumulative supplement, as part of Chapter 6, § 15. A commentary on the appellate court opinion, by which the case was reversed is in the supplement, as part of Chapter 8, § 15C.

The corporate sponsorship rules were enacted in 1997. Obviously of great import in the fund-raising context, these rules are discussed in this cumulative supplement, as part of Chapter 6, § 17. Regulations to accompany this law, either proposed or final, are imminent.

There have been two other important developments pertaining to federal fund-raising law. One is the finalization of the regulations underlying the statutory law that requires disclosure and dissemination of exempt organizations' annual information returns and application for recognition of tax exemption. Suddenly, charities are coping in a world where much information about them, including information about their fund-raising efforts, is readily available to the public. These regulations are summarized in this cumulative supplement, as part of Chapter 6, § 22.

The other of these developments is the evolving definition of a *royalty* for tax purposes, triggered by litigation initiated by several organizations, most notably the Sierra Club. The various opinions are discussed in this cumulative supplement, as part of Chapter 6, § 6.

There are other fund-raising issues the IRS is currently pursuing, such as automobile donation and scrip programs. Just as this cumulative supplement was going to press, the IRS issued its Continuing Professional Education Text for Fiscal Year 2000. These topics are discussed in Chapter T of that publication; the chapter is reproduced as Appendix K. Also in this appendix is a summary of Chapter I of the IRS text, which pertains to fund-raising law issues arising out of the use of the internet.

The watchdog agencies continue to grumble about developments that are positive for the philanthropic sector (see Chapter 9) but with declining effect, as the impression is that these groups are becoming increasingly marginalized in the modern era, largely because of the dissemination of information by means of new technologies, principally the Internet. (This process was greatly enhanced when the regulations, noted above, encouraging the posting of annual returns and exemption applications on the Internet, were approved in final form.) Speaking of which, the standoff between fund-raising charities and state regulators continues, with no governmental authority wanting to be the first to take the position that compliance with the state charitable solicitation acts is triggered by the raising of funds by means of that medium (see Chapter 8, § 15B).

As is the case in the nonprofit realm generally, it appears that much law and regulation lies ahead for the fund-raising community.

*December 1999*                                           BRUCE R. HOPKINS

# Supplement Contents

**Note to the Reader:** Materials new to this supplement are indicated by an asterisk (*) in the left margin of the contents below and throughout the supplement. Sections not in the main volume are indicated by "(New)" after the title.

# CONTENTS

# CONTENTS

# CONTENTS

# CHAPTER ONE

# Government Regulation of Fund-Raising for Charity: Origins and the Future

§ 1.1    The Independent Sector and American Political Philosophy
* § 1.2    The Independent Sector Today

## § 1.1    THE INDEPENDENT SECTOR AND AMERICAN POLITICAL PHILOSOPHY

p. 2, n. 4, second paragraph, line 2. *Replace "6th ed." with "7th ed."*

p. 2, n. 4, second paragraph, line 3. *Replace "1992" with "1998".*

## * §1.2    THE INDEPENDENT SECTOR TODAY

p. 9. *Insert as first complete paragraph after carryover paragraph:*

Five years later, these statistics were dramatically different. Americans contributed $174.52 billion to charitable organizations in 1998.[25.1] This was a 10.7 percent increase over the amount given ($157.59 billion) in 1997. This development marked the third straight year in which there was a dramatic increase in giving. The sources of contributions are as follows: individuals, $134.84 billion; foundations, $17.09 billion; bequests, $13.62 billion; and corporations, $8.97 billion. The charitable dollars were allocated as follows: religion, $76.06 billion; education, $24.56 billion; health, $16.89 billion; human services, $16.08 billion; public/society benefit, $10.86 billion; arts, culture,

[25.1] *Giving USA* (1999).

■  1  ■

and humanities, $10.53 billion; environmental/wildlife, $5.25 billion; international affairs, $2.14 billion; and noncorporate foundations, $16.94 billion.

# CHAPTER TWO

# The Anatomy of Charitable Fund-Raising

§ 2.1  Scope of the Term *Charitable* Organization

## § 2.1  SCOPE OF THE TERM *CHARITABLE* ORGANIZATION

p. 21, n. 4. *Replace "72-77, 100-108" with "§§ 5.1, 5.2".*

p. 22, n. 7. *Replace "123-127" with "§ 6.1".*

p. 22, n. 8. *Replace "127-129" with "§ 6.4".*

p. 22, n. 9. *Replace "129-132" with "§ 6.5".*

p. 22, n. 10. *Replace "132-135" with "§ 6.3".*

p. 22, n. 11. *Replace "135" with "138".*

p. 22, n. 12. *Replace "136-149" with "§ 6.2".*

p. 22, n. 13. *Replace "150-153" with "§ 6.6".*

p. 22, n. 14. *Replace "174-175" with "§ 6.10".*

p. 22, n. 15. *Replace "175" with "§ 6.10(b)".*

p. 22, n. 16. *Replace "176" with "§ 6.10(f)".*

p. 22, n. 17. *Replace "176" with "§ 6.10(f)".*

p. 22, n. 18. *Replace "176" with "§ 6.10(f)".*

p. 22, n. 19. *Replace "175-176" with "§ 6.10(c)"; replace "246-248" with "§ 10.2".*

p. 22, n. 21. *Replace "177-199" with "Chapter 7".*

p. 22, n. 22. *Replace "200-232" with "Chapter 8".*

p. 22, n. 23. *Replace "233-239" with "Chapter 9".*

p. 22, n. 24. *Replace "648-664, 693-704" with "§§ 18.11, 18.12, and 18.13, and Chapter 14"; replace "169-174, 704-711" with "§§ 6.9, 18.17".*

p. 22, n. 26. *Replace "549-571" with "Chapter 12".*

p. 23, n. 27. *Replace "616-621" with "§ 15.1".*

p. 23, n. 28. *Replace "572-596" with "Chapter 13".*

p. 23, n. 29. *Replace "597-615" with "Chapter 14".*

p. 23, n. 30. *Replace "672-676" with "§ 18.4".*

p. 23, n. 31. *Replace "690-693" with "§ 18.10".*

p. 23, n. 32. *Replace "648-664" with "Chapter 17".*

p. 23, n. 36. *Replace "355-545" with "Chapter 11".*

p. 23, n. 39. *Replace "200-232, 364" with "Chapter 8 and § 11.3(a)".*

p. 23, n. 40. *Replace "177-199, 364-366" with "Chapter 7 and § 11.3(a)".*

p. 23, n. 41. *Replace "136-149, 366-367" with "§§ 6.2, 11.3(a)".*

p. 23, n. 42. *Replace "369-387" with "§ 11.3(b)".*

# CHAPTER THREE

# The State Charitable Solicitation Acts: Comprehensive Summaries

p. 53, first full paragraph. *In first sentence, delete "Thirty-five" and substitute "Thirty-six".*

p. 53, n. 1. *Insert "Alabama," before existing text.*

p. 53, first full paragraph. *In second sentence, delete "Three" and substitute "Two".*

p. 53, n. 2. *Delete and substitute:*

Montana and Wyoming.

p. 53, n. 3. *Delete and substitute:*

Arizona, Delaware, District of Columbia, Idaho, Indiana, Iowa, Louisiana, Nebraska, Nevada, New Mexico, North Dakota, and Texas.

p. 53, first full paragraph. *In last sentence, delete "46" and substitute "49".*

## § 3.1   ALABAMA

pp. 53–55. *Replace section with:*

## Introduction

Comprehensive statute: Yes
Regulatory office: Attorney general
Citation: Ala. Code § 13A-9-70 *et seq.*

## Registration or Licensing Requirements

*Charitable Organizations.* A charitable organization, unless exempt from the requirement, may not lawfully solicit contributions in the state unless, prior to any solicitation, the organization has registered with the state's attorney general. This is done by filing a registration statement.

The registration statement must contain the following information: (1) the name of the charitable organization involved; (2) the name or names under which it intends to solicit contributions; (3) the names and addresses of the directors, trustees, officers, and executive personnel of the organization; (4) the address of the organization and the addresses of any offices in the state (or otherwise the name and address of the person having custody of its financial records; (5) the place where and the date when the organization was legally established; (6) the form of the organization; (7) the tax-exempt status of the organization; (8) the purposes for which the organization is organized; (9) the purpose or purposes for which the contributions to be solicited will be used; (10) the date on which the fiscal year of the organization ends; (11) whether the organization is authorized by any governmental authority to solicit contributions and whether it is or has ever been enjoined by any court from soliciting contributions; and (12) the names and addresses of any professional fund-raisers and commercial co-venturers who are acting or have agreed to act on behalf of the organization.

With the initial registration only, every charitable organization required to be registered must also file (1) a copy of the document by which it is organized; (2) a copy of its bylaws; (3) a statement setting forth the place where and the date when the organization was legally established, the form of the organization, and its tax-exempt status; and (4) a copy of any federal or state determination letters with respect to tax-exempt status.

This registration remains in effect until canceled or withdrawn. A registered organization must notify the attorney general within 10 days of any change in the information required to be furnished by the organization as part of the registration process.

*Professional Fund-Raisers.* A person may not act as a professional fund-raiser for a charitable organization without first registering with the attorney general. This registration is effective for a period of one year, expiring on September 30, and may be renewed for additional one-year periods. A person may not act as a professional fund-raiser after the expiration or cancellation of the registration, or prior to any renewal of it.

A professional fund-raiser must file, and have approved by the attorney general, a bond in the amount of $10,000.

*Professional Solicitors.* A person may not act as a professional solicitor in the employ of a professional fund-raiser who is required to register (see above) without first registering with the attorney general.

*Commercial Co-Venturers.* A person may not act as a commercial co-venturer with respect to a charitable organization without first registering with the attorney general. This registration is effective for a period of one year, expiring on September 30, and may be renewed for additional one-year periods. A person may not act as a commercial co-venturer after the expiration or cancellation of the registration, or prior to any renewal of it.

A commercial co-venturer must file, and have approved by the attorney general, a bond in the amount of $10,000.

## Reporting Requirements

*Charitable Organizations.* Every charitable organization required to register (see above) must file an annual written report. This report must contain (1) a financial statement, setting forth the gross income, expenses, and net income of the organization, and a balance sheet; and (2) a schedule of program activities carried on by the organization during the year and the associated expenditures. This requirement may be satisfied by the filing of a copy of the organization's federal annual information return.

This report is due within 90 days of the close of the organization's fiscal year. The attorney general is empowered to extend the time for filing a report for a period not in excess of 180 days.

*Professional Fund-Raisers.* There is no separate annual reporting requirement for professional fund-raisers. However, the effect of the annual registration requirement (see above) is the same as annual reporting.

A professional fund-raiser must, within 10 days after termination of a contract with a charitable organization (see below), file a closing statement with the attorney general disclosing gross receipts and all expenditures incurred in the performance of the contract.

*Professional Solicitors.* There is no separate annual reporting requirement for professional solicitors. However, the effect of the annual registration requirement (see above) is the same as annual reporting.

*Commercial Co-Venturers.* A commercial co-venturer must, within 10 days after termination of a contract with a charitable organization (see below), file a closing statement with the attorney general disclosing gross receipts and all expenditures incurred in the performance of the contract.


## Exemptions

There are no exemptions from the totality of this law. There are exemptions from the registration requirements for (1) educational institutions and their "authorized and related" foundations; (2) religious organizations; (3) political organizations; (4) fraternal, patriotic, benevolent, social, educational, alumni, health care foundation, historical, and civil rights organizations, including fraternities and sororities and any auxiliaries associated with these organizations; (5) civic leagues and civic organizations that solicit contributions solely from their own membership; (6) persons requesting contributions for the relief of a named individual when the gifts do not exceed $10,000 and are turned over in their entirety to the beneficiary; (7) a charitable organization that does not receive contributions in excess of $25,000 in a year, as long as all of the fund-raising functions are carried on by volunteers; (8) qualified charitable organizations receiving an allocation from an incorporated community chest or united fund; (9) a local post, camp, chapter, or similarly designated element, or a county unit of such elements, of a bona fide veterans' organization, which issues charters to local elements in the state, or a bona fide auxiliary or affiliate of these organizations, as long as all of the fund-raising functions are carried on by members of the organization or their family members or by other volunteers; and (10) a bona fide organization of volunteer firefighters, ambulance companies, or rescue squads, or a bona fide auxiliary or affiliate of these organizations, as long as all of the fund-raising functions are carried on by members of the organization or their family members or by other volunteers.

## Commercial Co-Venturers

The law in this state applies to commercial co-venturers. The requirements involved are registration and bonding (see above), and rules as to contracts (see below). A *commercial co-venturer* is defined as any "person who for profit or other commercial consideration, conducts, promotes, underwrites, arranges, or sponsors a sale, performance, or event of any kind which is advertised, and which will benefit, to any extent, a charitable or religious organization." This definition does not encompass a person who benefits in good will only where the collection and distribution of the proceeds of the sale, performance, or event are supervised and controlled by the beneficiary charitable or religious organization.

## Other Requirements

*Contracts.*   All contracts between professional fund-raisers or commercial co-venturers and charitable organizations must be in writing. A "true and correct" copy of each contract must be filed by the professional fund-raiser or commercial co-venturer with the attorney general within 10 days following execution. Services may not be performed under a contract until the expiration of 15 days from the date the contract is filed with the attorney general.

*Record Keeping and Accounting.*   All records, books, and reports maintained by a charitable organization registered or required to register under this law (see above) must be available for inspection, during normal business hours at the principal office of the organization, by the office of the attorney general.

A professional fund-raiser or commercial co-venturer must maintain accurate and current books and records while required to be registered (see above), for at least two years. These items must be available for inspection by the office of the attorney general.

## Unique Provisions

*Disclosures.*   An individual "in the process of soliciting funds shall identify himself or herself." If the individual is being paid for soliciting, the solicitee must be so informed. This information must be disclosed to the solicitee "in a clear manner before attempting any solicitations."

*Prohibited Acts.* A person—other than a director, trustee, or officer of a charitable organization by or for which contributions are solicited—may not, for the purposes of soliciting contributions in the state, use the name of a charitable organization without the consent of the organization. This includes listing the organization's name on any stationery, advertisement, brochure, or correspondence in or by which a contribution is solicited.

A charitable organization or professional fund-raiser soliciting contributions may not use a name, symbol, or statement so closely related or similar to that used by another charitable organization or governmental agency that the use would tend to confuse or mislead the public.

*Other.* Provision is made for the deemed appointment of the secretary of state as agent for service of process on behalf of an out-of-state charitable organization, professional fund-raiser, professional solicitor, or commercial co-venturer.

## Sanctions

The attorney general must cancel the registration of any charitable organization that fails within the time prescribed to comply with this law, or fails to furnish any additional information requested by the attorney general within the required time.

A person who knowingly violates this law is guilty of charitable fraud. An initial violation of this law constitutes a misdemeanor; subsequent violations are felonies.

The attorney general or a district attorney may bring an action to enjoin a violation of this law. A failure to discontinue a charitable solicitation when requested to do so by the attorney general or to register (see above) may result in a penalty not in excess of $5,000.

A professional fund-raiser or professional solicitor who commits both of the following acts is guilty of theft of property by charitable fraud: (1) knowingly represents that he or she is soliciting funds for a charitable organization, without the organization's consent; and (2) receives any contributions that are not delivered to the charitable organization within 30 days of receipt or within 10 days following request for them by the organization, whichever is sooner.

The attorney general, the district attorneys of the counties in the state, or an affected charitable organization may bring an action against a charitable organization, professional fund-raiser, professional solicitor, or commercial co-venturer, and any persons acting on their behalf, to enjoin the charitable organization and other persons from continuing a charitable solicitation. The purpose of this type of action may also be to cancel a registration. These actions can be maintained when there is reason to believe that the charitable organization (1) operated in violation of this law; (2) refused or failed, or any of its principal officers refused or failed, after notice, to produce any records of the charitable organization; (3) engaged in, or is about to engage in, any charitable solicitation through the use of any scheme or plan, including any device or artifice, to defraud, or for obtaining money or property by means of false pretense, representation, or promises; or (4) made, or is making, a material false statement in an application, registration, or statement required to be filed pursuant to this law.

A charitable organization, professional fund-raiser, professional solicitor, commercial co-venturer, their agents, or any other person who violates the terms of an injunction or other order entered under this law must, in addition to other remedies, forfeit and pay to the state a civil penalty of not more than $25,000 for each violation. In the case of a violation through "continuing failure or neglect" to obey the order, each day of continuance of the failure or neglect is deemed a separate offense.

Upon a finding that any person has engaged in or is engaging in an act or practice declared unlawful by this law, the court may make any necessary order or judgment, including injunctions, restitution, awards of reasonable attorneys' fees, and costs of investigation and litigation, and may award to the state civil penalties up to $5,000 for each violation of this law. In requesting injunctive relief, the attorney general or district attorney is not required to establish irreparable harm but only that a violation has occurred or that the requested order promotes the public interest.

## § 3.8 DELAWARE

p. 79. *Replace section with:*

## Introduction

Comprehensive statute: No
Regulatory office: Attorney general
Citation: Delaware Code, tit. 6, ch. 25, subch. IX

## Registration or Licensing Requirements

*Charitable Organizations.* This statute does not contain any registration requirements for charitable organizations.

*Professional Fund-Raisers.* This statute does not contain any registration requirements for professional fund-raisers.

*Professional Solicitors.* This statute does not contain any registration requirements for professional solicitors.

## Reporting Requirements

*Charitable Organizations.* This statute does not contain any reporting requirements for charitable organizations.

*Professional Fund-Raisers.* This statute does not contain any reporting requirements for professional fund-raisers.

*Professional Solicitors.* This statute does not contain any reporting requirements for professional solicitors.

## Exemptions

This statute does not contain any exemptions.

## Commercial Co-Venturers

This statute does not regulate commercial co-ventures.

## Other Requirements

*Contracts.* There must be a written contract between a charitable organization and a professional solicitor. The contract must clearly state the respective obligations of the parties and the compensation terms of the professional solicitor. This contract must be kept for at least three years following its termination.

A professional solicitor is required to review the requirements of this law prior to executing a contract with a charitable organization.

*Record Keeping and Accounting.* A professional solicitor must keep accurate fiscal records regarding its charitable solicitations in the state. These records must be kept for at least three years following the termination of a contract with a charitable organization (see above).

## Unique Provisions

*Disclosures.* See Prohibited Acts (below).

*Prohibited Acts.* It is an unlawful practice for any person to engage in any deception, fraud, false pretense, false promise, or misrepresentation, or to conceal, suppress, or omit any material fact with the intent that others rely on the concealment, suppression, or omission, in connection with a charitable solicitation, whether or not any person has in fact been misled, deceived, or damaged by a practice.

These practices include (1) the failure of an individual to identify himself or herself by name prior to making a charitable solicitation; (2) the failure of a person to identify the charitable organization for which the solicitation is being made or the purpose of the solicitation prior to making the solicitation; (3) if the solicitation is made by a professional solicitor, the failure to disclose that the person soliciting the contribution is, or is employed by, a professional solicitor and the identity of the professional solicitor; (4) upon request by the solicitee, the failure of any person to disclose the amount or percentage of the contribution that will be turned over to the charitable organization, the amount or percentage of the contribution to be used for the charitable purposes for which it was solicited, or the amount or percentage to be retained by the professional solicitor (except that when the amount or percentage to be turned over to the charitable organization is not known at the time of the solicitation, there shall be a good faith estimate of that amount or percentage); (5) the use or reference to the term "police," "law enforcement," "trooper," "rescue squad," "fireman," or "firefighter," unless (a) the person making the representation is employed by a bona fide police, law enforcement, rescue squad, or fire department and the person is authorized by the entity to engage in charitable solicitation, or (b) the entity has authorized the use or reference to the term in writing for the purpose of charitable solicitation; (6) the representation that a percentage of the contribution will be used for a charitable purpose if the person has reason to believe that is not the case; (7) the representation that another person endorses the solicitation, unless that person has consented in writing to the use of the person's name for the purpose of endorsing the solicitation; (8) the representation that the contribution is solicited on behalf of anyone other than the charitable organization that authorized the solicitation; (9) the use of the name of a charitable organization without the written consent of the organization; (10) the use of a name, symbol, or statement so closely related or similar to that used by another charitable organization or governmental agency that the use would tend to confuse or mislead the public; (11) the failure to create and/or maintain the records and written contracts as required by this law (see above) with the intent to hinder the discovery of practices otherwise prohibited by this law or having otherwise been in violation of these rules; (12) and the failure to comply with the time restriction rules (see below) on three separate occasions.

*Other.* A charitable organization or any director, officer, member, volunteer, or employee of a charitable organization may not be deemed in violation of this law for an unlawful practice committed by a professional solicitor unless the organization or individual has actual prior knowledge of, or had fraudulent intent in connection with, the unlawful practice.

A charitable organization or professional solicitor may not engage in charitable solicitation of any person after 9:00 P.M. or before 8:00 A.M., unless authorized by the solicitee prior to the solicitation.

The purpose of this law is stated to be to "safeguard the public against fraudulent and misleading charitable solicitations, thereby enhancing public confidence in legitimate charitable . . . organizations."

### Sanctions

The sanctions for violation of this law are stated in other statutes of the state. The remedies and penalties provided for in this law are not exclusive and are in addition to any other procedures, rights, or remedies which exist with respect to any other provisions of law, including state and/or federal criminal prosecutions and/or actions brought by private parties.

## § 3.12 HAWAII

### Registration or Licensing Requirements

pp. 97–99. *Replace Charitable Organizations subsection with:*

*Charitable Organizations.* As of July 1, 1996, there are no registration or licensing requirements applicable to charitable organizations.

**Reporting Requirements**

*Charitable Organizations.*

p. 99, first paragraph. *Delete second sentence.*

**Exemptions**

p. 100. *Delete subsection.*

**Other Requirements**

*Other.*

p. 102, carryover paragraph. *Replace first full sentence with:*

The department is empowered to grant an exemption from the annual registration requirement to a charitable organization operating in another state, where the organization's funds are derived principally from sources outside the state and the other organization is exempt from the registration requirements of the law of the other state, as long as the other state's law is similar to this law.

**Unique Provisions**

*Other.*

p. 103. *Delete first paragraph of subsection.*

## § 3.25 MISSISSIPPI

**Registration or Licensing Requirements**

p. 160. *Replace item (11) with:*

(11) a statement as to whether the organization is authorized by any other governmental authority to solicit contributions; (12) a statement as to whether the organization or any of its directors, officers, or executive

personnel has had a license or registration denied, suspended, revoked, or enjoined by a court or other governmental authority in any state, or whether the organization has voluntarily entered into an assurance or voluntary discontinuance or agreement with any jurisdiction or federal agency or officer;

p. 161, line 7. *Delete "and".*

p. 161, line 8. *Insert before period:*

; (18) a financial report; (19) with the initial registration only, a copy of the document by which the organization was created and its bylaws; and (20) with the initial registration or, after registration, within 30 days of its receipt, a copy of any federal determination letter as to tax-exempt status, any determination revoking the organization's federal exempt status, or any communication from the IRS concerning a challenge to or investigation of the organization's ongoing classification as a tax-exempt organization.

p. 161, end of fourth paragraph. *Replace "$25,000" with "$10,000".*

## Reporting Requirements

p. 161, next-to-last paragraph, line 2. *Replace "$50,000" with "$100,000"; insert "fiscal" following "any".*

p. 161, next-to-last paragraph, line 3. *Delete "(ending June 30)".*

p. 161, next-to-last paragraph, lines 5–6. *Replace "the immediately preceding 12-month period of operation" with "its most recently completed fiscal year".*

p. 161, next-to-last paragraph, lines 10–11. *Replace with:*

public; and (8) total net amount disbursed or dedicated for

p. 161, last paragraph. *Delete first sentence.*

p. 162. *Add to carryover paragraph:*

This report must be accompanied by "any and all forms required to be filed by a charitable organization" with the IRS.

p. 162, line 5. *Replace "12-month period (ending June 30)" with "fiscal year";
replace "$50,000" with "$100,000".*

p. 162, lines 7–14. *Replace with:*

must file a written report with the secretary of state. This report must include
a financial statement covering the most recently completed fiscal year, including a statement of the organization's gross receipts from and use of contributions. This report must be accompanied by "any and all forms required to be
filed by a charitable organization" with the IRS.

A charitable organization that receives more than $25,000 but less than
$100,000 must, at the request of the secretary, submit financial information,
including an audited financial statement accompanied by an opinion signed by
an independent certified public accountant that the financial statement "fairly
represents the financial operations of the organization in sufficient detail to
permit public evaluation of its operations."

p. 162, third complete paragraph. *Replace with:*

*Professional Fund-Raisers.* The annual registration requirement (see
above) serves as the equivalent of an annual reporting requirement.

In addition, prior to the commencement of a solicitation, a professional
fund-raiser must file a report with the secretary containing information about
the following: (1) the fund-raising methods to be used; (2) the projected dates
when the solicitation will commence and terminate; (3) the location and telephone number from where the solicitation will be conducted if it is to be done
by telephone; (4) the name and residence address of each person responsible
for directing and supervising the conduct of the solicitation; (5) a statement as
to whether the professional fund-raiser will at any time have custody of any
contributions; (6) the account number and location of each bank account
where receipts from the solicitation are to be deposited; (7) a "full and fair"
description of the charitable program for which the solicitation is being carried out, and (8) the written and signed consent of every charitable organization on behalf of which the professional fund-raiser will be soliciting
contributions or the name of which will be mentioned during the solicitation.
The secretary is empowered to promulgate rules requiring additional information.

Also see Accounting (below).

THE STATE CHARITABLE SOLICITATION ACTS

## Exemptions

p. 162, last paragraph, lines 1–6. *Replace with:*

This statute is inapplicable to (1) a religious organization which is tax-exempt under federal law and is primarily supported by gifts from its membership or congregation, program service revenue, or government grants or contracts; (2) an educational institution that is recognized by the

p. 162, last paragraph, line 7. *Replace "(4)" with "(3)".*

p. 162, last paragraph, line 8. *Replace "(5)" with "(4)".*

p. 162, last paragraph, line 9. *Replace "(6)" with "(5)".*

p. 162, last paragraph, line 11. *Replace "(7)" with "(6)".*

p. 162, last paragraph, line 12. *Replace "(8)" with "(7)".*

p. 163, line 1. *Replace "(9)" with "(8)".*

p. 163, line 6. *Replace "(10)" with "(9)".*

p. 163, line 9. *Replace "(11)" with "(10)".*

p. 163, line 10. *Replace "(12)" with "(11)".*

p. 163, line 11. *Insert "or rescue units" following "department".*

p. 163, line 12. *Add to carryover paragraph:*

; (12) a humane society organized under state law which contracts with counties or municipalities for the "care and keeping of estrays"; and (13) any other organization which the secretary exempts (but only from the registration requirements) upon a finding that (a) the registration is not necessary in the public interest or for the protection of contributors or (b) the exemption furthers the "objectives of compatibility with uniformity among the states."

p. 163. *Add after first full paragraph:*

Prior to a solicitation for contributions, a charitable organization claiming to be exempt must file a notice of exemption with the secretary. The burden of proving the availability of an exemption or an exception from a definition is upon the person claiming it.

**Other Requirements**

p. 163. *Insert following third full paragraph:*

The contract must contain the following provisions: (1) the legal name and address of the charitable organization; (2) a statement of the charitable purpose for which the solicitation campaign is being conducted; (3) a statement of the respective obligations of the professional fund-raiser and the charitable organization; (4) a "clear" statement of the fees or rate that will be paid to the professional fund-raiser; (5) the effective and termination dates of the contract; (6) the date services will commence with respect to the solicitation of contributions in the state; and (7) a statement that the charitable organization exercises control and approval over the content and volume of any solicitation. The secretary is empowered to promulgate rules requiring additional items in these contracts.

p. 163, next-to-last paragraph, line 2. *Replace "accurate and detailed" with:*

true and correct

p. 163. *Insert following fourth full paragraph:*

During each solicitation, and for at least three years after the completion of it, the professional fund-raiser must maintain the following records (which must be made available to the attorney general or the secretary upon request): (1) a record of each contribution that at any time is in the custody of the professional fund-raiser, including the name and address of each contributor and the date and amount of the contribution; and (2) the location of each financial institution in which the professional fund-raiser has deposited revenue from the solicitation and the account number of each account into which deposits were made.

Within 90 days of completion of a solicitation and on any anniversary of the commencement of a solicitation, the professional fund-raiser must furnish an accounting of all contributions collected and expenses paid to the charitable organization with which the professional fund-raiser has contracted. This accounting must be retained by the parties for three years. A final report of the accounting must be filed by the professional fund-raiser with the secretary.

Within two days after the receipt of a contribution, the professional fund-raiser must deposit the entire amount of the contribution in an account at a federally insured financial institution, which must be in the name of the charitable organization. The charitable entity must have sole control of all withdrawals from the account.

Any material change in any of this information filed with the secretary must be reported by the professional fund-raiser to the secretary within seven days of the change.

**Unique Provisions**

p. 163. *Insert before last paragraph:*

*Disclosures.* Prior to orally requesting a contribution or contemporaneously with written requests for a contribution, a professional fund-raiser and professional solicitor are responsible for "clearly and conspicuously" disclosing (1) the name of the professional fund-raiser as on file with the secretary; (2) the fact that the solicitation is being conducted by a professional fund-raiser who is being compensated; (3) the legal name of the professional solicitor (if the solicitor is identified by name); (4) the name of the charitable organization as on file with the secretary; and (5) how the contributions raised by the solicitation will be utilized for a charitable purpose. All responses given in response to a request for information must be truthful. Any written confirmation, receipt, or reminder sent to a person who has contributed or has pledged to contribute, in response to an oral solicitation, must include a "clear and conspicuous" disclosure of this information.

There is a legend requirement.

*Percentages.* If requested by the person being solicited, a professional fund-raiser or professional solicitor must inform that person orally, and also in writing within 14 days of the request, of the "fixed percentage of the gross revenue" or a reasonable estimate of the percentage of gross revenue that the charitable organization will receive as the result of the solicitation.

p. 163. *Replace last three lines with:*

*Prohibited Acts.* A person may not (1) misrepresent the purpose or beneficiary of a solicitation; (2) misrepresent the purpose or nature of a charitable organization; (3) use or exploit the fact of registration so as to lead the public to believe that the registration constitutes an endorsement or approval by the state; (4) misrepresent that another person sponsors or endorses a solicitation; (5) use the name of a charitable organization, or display an emblem, device, or printed matter belonging to or associated with a charitable organization without the express written permission of the charitable organization; (6) make a false or misleading statement on a document required by this law; (7) fail to comply with this law; (8) commit an unfair or deceptive act or practice; (9) fail to provide complete and timely payment to a charitable organization of the proceeds from a solicitation; (10) employ a device, scheme, or artifice to defraud; (11) make any false or misleading statements in the solicitation of contributions in the state or to omit to state any fact necessary in order to make the statements made, in light of the circumstances in which they are made, not misleading; (12) engage in any act, practice, or course of business that operates or would operate as a fraud or deceit upon any person; (13) refuse or fail, after notice, to produce any records required to be kept under this law; (14) obtain money or property by means of any false pretense, representation, or promise; or (15) violate any provision of this law.

A charitable organization may not (1) engage in any financial transaction that is not related to the accomplishment of its charitable purpose, or which jeopardizes or interferes with the ability of the charitable organization to accomplish its charitable purpose; (2) expend an unreasonable amount of money for solicitation or management; (3) use a name which is the same as or confusingly similar to the name of another charitable organization unless the latter entity consents in writing to the use; (4) represent itself as being associated with another charitable organization without the express written acknowledgment and endorsement of the other charitable entity; (5) use the services of an unregistered professional fund-raiser or professional solicitor; or (6) violate a provision of this law.

A professional fund-raiser or professional solicitor may not perform any services on behalf of an unregistered charitable organization or otherwise violate this law.

p. 164. *Delete lines 1–14.*

p. 164. *Delete fourth full paragraph.*

p. 164. *Insert following seventh paragraph:*

A person who solicits, collects, or expends contributions on behalf of a charitable organization or otherwise for a charitable purpose, and every trustee, director, officer, or employee of that person who is concerned with the solicitation, collection, or expenditure of contributions, is considered a fiduciary and as acting in a fiduciary capacity.

A professional fund-raiser or professional solicitor involved in a solicitation on behalf of a charitable organization by telephone, to residential numbers, may make calls only between the hours of 9:00 A.M. and 9:00 P.M. Moreover, telephone calls may not be made on Sundays.

p. 164. *Replace last two lines with:*

The secretary must deny, suspend, or revoke a registration or an exemption if (1) the application for it is incomplete; (2) the application or renewal fee (if applicable) has not been paid; (3) a document filed with the secretary contains one or more false or misleading statements or omits material facts; (4) the charitable contributions have not been or are not being applied for the purpose or purposes stated in documents filed with the secretary; (5) the applicant or registrant has violated or failed to comply with this law; (6) the applicant, registrant, officers, directors, or partners of the applicant or registrant, or their agents or employees, have been convicted of any felony or misdemeanor where the matter involved misrepresentation, misapplication, or misuse of the property of another; (7) the applicant or registrant has engaged in the use or employment of dishonesty, fraud, deception, misrepresentation, false promise, or false pretense; (8) the applicant or registrant has had the authority to engage in charitable or fund-raising activities denied, revoked, or suspended by the secretary or other jurisdiction; (9) the applicant or registrant has been convicted of a variety of criminal offenses; or (10) the applicant or registrant has engaged in other forms of misconduct as may be determined by rules promulgated by the secretary.

Where it appears to the secretary that a violation of this law has occurred or is about to occur, the secretary may (in addition to other remedies authorized by law) (1) issue a cease-and-desist order directing those involved to cease and desist from further illegal activity or (2) issue an order imposing an administrative penalty up to $25,000 for each offense.

The attorney general of the state is accorded broad authority to conduct investigations in the enforcement of this law. Where it appears to the attorney general of the state that a person has violated or is about to violate this law, the attorney general may bring a court action to enjoin the acts involved. The court may issue a restraining order or writ of mandamus, and may appoint a receiver or conservator for the defendant or the defendant's assets. The court may enter an order of rescission, restitution, or disgorgement directed to a person who has violated this law. The court may impose a civil penalty up to $25,000 for each offense.

p. 165. *Delete first six lines.*

p. 165. *Add to second full paragraph:*

In connection with a solicitation, any person employing a device, scheme, or artifice to defraud, or engaging in any act, practice, or course of business that operates or would operate as a fraud or deceit upon any person, or obtaining money or property by means of any false pretense, representation, or promise is guilty of a felony and, upon conviction, shall be punished by a fine not in excess of $25,000 or imprisoned up to five years, or both. An indictment or information may not be returned under this law more than five years after the alleged violation.

## § 3.30 NEW HAMPSHIRE

**Unique Provisions**

*Other.*

p. 176. *Insert after third full paragraph:*

A charitable organization must adopt a conflict of interest policy and a policy concerning "pecuniary benefit transactions" before it solicits contributions in the state. The latter generally is a transaction with a charitable organization in which a trustee, director, or officer of the organization has, directly or indirectly, a financial interest. A pecuniary benefit transaction is prohibited unless a variety of conditions are met, including approval of the transaction by a two-thirds majority of the board of the organization and maintenance of a list of these transactions available to the organization's membership and donors. If the transaction involves at least $5,000, the organization must publish notice of it in a newspaper of general circulation in its community or the state. A copy of these policies, and any subsequent modifications of them, must be filed with the state.

## § 3.34 NORTH CAROLINA

**Registration or Licensing Requirements**

*Charitable Organizations.*

p. 196. *Insert after carryover paragraph:*

As to item (22), if the charitable organization has not received a determination as to federal tax-exempt status as of the time of initial licensing, a copy of the determination must be filed with the department within 30 days of its receipt. If the organization is subsequently notified by the IRS of any challenge to its "continued entitlement" to federal tax exemption, the organization is required to notify the department of this fact within 30 days after receipt.

**Unique Provisions**

*Disclosures.*

p. 200. *Add to last paragraph:*

This mode of disclosure was modified in 1996 to, among other outcomes, eliminate the requirement that the legend appear in capital letters.

## § 3.43   TENNESSEE

**Registration or Licensing Requirements**

p. 252, first full paragraph. *In first line insert "initial" following "The".*

p. 252, first full paragraph. *Replace item (9) with:*

(9) a statement as to whether the organization intends to solicit contributions directly from the public or have such done on its behalf by others; (10) a copy of any agreement with a fund-raising counsel, professional solicitor, or any other person who is directly or indirectly involved with the solicitation of contributions; (11) a statement as to whether the organization is authorized by any other governmental authority to solicit contributions; (12) a statement as to whether the organization is or has ever been enjoined by any court from soliciting contributions; (13) the general purpose or purposes for which the contributions to be solicited are to be used; (14) the name or names under which the organization intends to solicit contributions; (15) the names of the individuals who will have final responsibility for the custody of the contributions; (16) the names of the individuals responsible for the final distribution of the contributions; and (17) a statement as to whether any director, officer, manager, operator, or principal of the organization has been the subject of an injunction, judgment, or administrative order or has been convicted of a felony.

During its first year of operation, a newly registered charitable organization must provide quarterly financial reports, due within 30 days after the end of each quarter of its fiscal year, containing (1) the gross amount of contributions received; (2) the amount of contributions disbursed or to be disbursed to each charitable organization or charitable purposes represented; (3) the aggregate amounts paid to any professional fund-raiser or professional solicitor; and (4) the amounts spent for overhead, expenses, commissions, and similar purposes.

An organization that has applied for but not received a determination as to recognition of its tax-exempt status from the IRS must file a copy of the completed application submitted to the IRS, as well as any letters from the IRS acknowledging receipt of the application.

p. 252, third full paragraph, second line. *Replace "$5,000" with "$30,000".*

p. 252, third full paragraph, fourth line. *Replace "$5,000" with "$30,000".*

p. 252. *Insert after fifth full paragraph:*

A renewal of registration must be accompanied by a copy of a financial statement, identifying the amount of funds raised and related expenses, all publicity costs, and costs of allocation or disbursement of funds raised. The secretary is empowered to accept a copy of the organization's federal annual information return and must require other information and documentation to describe how funds were raised and spent to substantiate the figures on the reported return, including an accountant's statement and proof that the return submitted to the secretary was in fact filed with the IRS.

The annual report of a charitable organization that received in excess of $100,000 in gross revenue during its most recently completed fiscal year must be accompanied by an audited financial statement, presented in accordance with generally accepted accounting principles, which has been examined by an independent certified public accountant for the purpose of expressing an opinion on it. The annual report of a charitable organization receiving more than $25,000 but less than $100,000 must be filed and accompanied by any and all of the forms required to be filed by a charitable organization with the IRS. At the request of the secretary, an organization in this latter category must submit an audited financial statement, presented in accordance with generally accepted accounting principles, which has been examined by an independent certified public accountant.

A person that ceases solicitation activities after registration must notify the secretary of that fact within 30 days after solicitation activities end. Financial documentation must be filed by a person in these circumstances within 90 days after the end of the solicitation activities or 90 days after the close of its fiscal year.

**Exemptions**

p. 253, third-to-last line. *Replace "$5,000" with "$30,000".*

p. 253. *Insert after last paragraph:*

A charitable organization that claims to be exempt from the registration requirement and that intends to or does solicit charitable contributions must submit to the secretary a statement containing the organization's name, address, and purpose, as well as the reason for the claim for exemption.

## Unique Provisions

### *Disclosures.*

p. 256. *Insert after carryover paragraph:*

A person that intends to continue to solicit contributions after its registration anniversary date (see above) and fails to renew its registration or exemption by the time of the expiration or fails to request an extension of time is in violation of this law.

## Sanctions

p. 256. *Insert after second paragraph:*

Applications by charitable organizations for renewal of registration (see above) are assessed a late fee for each month or portion of a month that the application is not timely filed.

## § 3.45  UTAH

## Introduction

p. 259. *Replace last line with:*

Citation: Utah Code Ann. § 13-22-1 et seq. (1953)

## Registration or Licensing Requirements

### *Charitable Organizations.*

p. 260, first paragraph. *Replace with:*

A charitable organization, unless exempt from the requirement, may not solicit contributions in the state unless, prior to any solicitation, the organization has secured a permit from the state's division of consumer protection.

p. 260, second paragraph. *Replace item 1 of list with:*

(1) the organization's name, address, telephone number, any facsimile number, and the names and addresses of any persons controlled by, controlling, or affiliated with the organization;

p. 260, second paragraph. *Replace item 8 with:*

(8) the anticipated expenses of the solicitation;

p. 260, second paragraph. *Replace items 11–13 with:*

(11) the name and address of the registered agent for service of process and a consent to service of process; (12) a copy of any written agreements with any professional fund-raiser or professional solicitor involved with the solicitation; (13) disclosure of any injunction, judgment, or administrative order, or conviction of any crime involving moral turpitude with respect to any director, officer, manager, operator, or principal of the organization; (14) a copy of all agreements to which the organization is, or proposes to be, a party regarding the use of proceeds for fund-raising; (15) a statement as to whether the organization, or its parent foundation, will be using the services of a professional fund-raiser or a professional fund-raising counsel; (16) if either the organization or its parent foundation will be using the services of a professional fund-raiser or a professional fund-raising counsel, (a) a copy of all agreements related to the services; and (b) an acknowledgment that fund-raising in the state will not commence until the charitable organization, its parent foundation (if any), and the professional fund-raiser or professional fund-raising counsel are registered and in compliance with this law; and (17) any additional information the division may require by rule.

If any information contained in the application for registration becomes incorrect or incomplete, the organization must, within 30 days, correct the application or file the complete information required.

p. 260. *Replace third paragraph with:*

This registration expires annually on the earlier of January 1, April 1, July 1, or October 1 following the completion of 12 months after the date of its initial issuance, and is renewable.

pp. 260–261. *Replace Professional Fund-Raisers and Professional Solicitors subsections with:*

**Professional Fund-Raisers.**   A person may not, without first obtaining a professional fund-raiser's permit, provide fund-raising consulting or similar services with respect to a charitable purpose on behalf of any organization (whether or not it is exempt from registration) in exchange for compensation. However, this rule does not apply to an individual who is a bona fide officer or employee of a charitable organization that holds a permit, if the solicitation is solely for the benefit of that organization.

To obtain a permit as a professional fund-raiser (termed a *professional fund-raising counsel or consultant*), an applicant must submit an application that includes (1) the applicant's name, address, telephone number, and any facsimile number; (2) the name and address of any person controlled by, controlling, or affiliated with the applicant; (3) the applicant's business, occupation, or employment for the three-year period immediately preceding the date of the application; (4) the legal form of the applicant (such as individual, corporation, or joint venture); (5) the names and resident addresses of any directors or officers of the applicant; (6) the name and address of the registered agent for service of process and a consent to service of process; (7) disclosure of any injunction, judgment, or administrative order against the applicant or the applicant's conviction of any crime involving moral turpitude; (8) disclosure of any injunction, judgment, or administrative order or conviction of any crime involving moral turpitude with respect to any director, officer, manager, operator, or principal of the applicant; (9) a copy of any written agreements with the charitable organization involved; (10) a copy of all agreements to which the applicant is or proposes to be a party regarding the use of proceeds; (11) an acknowledgment that fund-raising in the state will not commence until the professional fund-raiser and the charitable organization (and any parent foundation) are registered and in compliance with this law; (12) the purpose of the plan, management, advice, counsel, or preparation of materials for or with respect to the solicitation and use of the contributions solicited; (13) the method by which the plan, management, advice, counsel, or preparation of materials for or with respect to the solicitation will be organized or coordinated and the projected length of time for the solicitation; (14) the anticipated expenses of the plan, management, advice, counsel, or preparation of materials for or with respect to the solicitation, including commissions, costs of collection, and salaries; (15) a statement of total fees to be earned or received from the charitable organization, and the percentage of the contributions collected as a result of the plan, management, advice, counsel, or preparation of materials for or with respect to the solicitation that is projected after deducting the total fees to be earned or received to remain available to the charitable organization, including a "satisfactory" statement of the factual basis for the projected percentage and projected anticipated revenues provided to the charitable organization, and if a flat fee is charged, documentation to support the reasonableness of the fee; (16) a statement of total net fees earned or received within the calendar year immediately preceding the date of application, including a description of the expenditures made from or the use of the net earned or received fees in the planning, management, advising, counseling, or preparation of materials for or with respect to the solicitation and use of the contributions solicited for the charitable organization; and (17) any additional information the division may require.

If any information in this application becomes incorrect or incomplete, the applicant must, within 30 days, correct the application or file the complete information required by the division.

This permit expires on the earlier of annually as of the date of issuance or when the professional fund-raiser ceases affiliation with the charitable organization involved, and is renewable.

An applicant must provide proof of a bond or provide a letter of credit in the amount of at least $25,000.

*Professional Solicitors.* A person may not, without first obtaining a professional solicitor's permit, solicit a contribution for a charitable purpose on behalf of any organization (whether or not it is registered) in exchange for compensation.

To obtain a permit as a professional solicitor (termed a *professional fund-raiser*), an applicant must submit an application that includes (1) the information and items referenced in (1)–(11) above (concerning the application filed by professional fund-raising counsel or consultants); (2) the purpose of the solicitation; (3) the use of the contributions to be solicited; (4) the method by which the solicitation will be conducted; (5) the projected length of time the solicitation is to be conducted; (6) the anticipated expenses of the solicitation, including commissions, costs of collection, and salaries; (7) a statement of the percentage of the contributions collected as a result of the solicitation that are projected to remain available to the charitable organization involved, including a "satisfactory" statement of the factual basis for the projected percentage and projected anticipated revenues provided to the charitable organization, and, if a flat fee is charged, documentation to support the reasonableness of the fee; (8) a statement of total contributions collected or received by the professional solicitor within the calendar year immediately preceding the date of the application, including a description of the expenditures made from or the use made of the contributions; and (9) any additional information the division may require.

If any information in this application becomes incorrect or incomplete, the applicant must, within 30 days, correct the application or file the complete information required by the division.

This permit expires on the earlier of annually as of the date of issuance or when the professional solicitor ceases affiliation with the charitable organization involved and is renewable.

An applicant must provide proof of a bond or provide a letter of credit in the amount of at least $25,000.

## Reporting Requirements

p. 261. *Replace first paragraph of subsection with:*

*Charitable Organizations.* The annual registration requirement (see above) serves as the equivalent of an annual reporting requirement. Also, after the first year of continuous registration, a charitable organization must file an annual financial report or a copy of its federal annual information return within 30 days after the end of the year involved.

A charitable organization registered under this law must, during its first year of registration, provide quarterly financial reports to the division within 30 days after the end of the quarter reported, disclosing (1) the gross amount of contributions received; (2) the amount of contributions disbursed or to be disbursed to each charitable organization or charitable purpose represented; (3) aggregate amounts paid to a professional solicitor; (4) amounts spent for overhead, expenses, commissions, and similar purposes; and (5) the name and address of any paid solicitor used by the organization.

## Exemptions

p. 261, first paragraph. *Replace items (1) and (2) with:*

(1) an organization that conducts a charitable solicitation among its "established and bona fide" membership exclusively through the volunteer efforts of its members and officers; (2) a "bona fide" religious, ecclesiastical, or denominational organization if (a) the solicitation is made for a church, missionary, religious, or humanitarian purpose, and (b) the organization is a church or similar entity, another type of bona fide tax-exempt religious organization, or certain other organizations that are integral parts of tax-exempt charitable institutions;

p. 261, first paragraph. *In line 7, insert following "individual":*

sustaining a life-threatening illness or injury

p. 261, first paragraph. *Replace items (6), (7), and (8) with:*

(6) a school accredited by the state or an accredited educational institution, or a club or parent, teacher, or student organization within and authorized by the school in support of the operations or extracurricular activities of the school; (7) certain public or higher education foundations; (8) a volunteer fire department, rescue squad, or local civil defense organization whose financial oversight is under the control of a local governmental entity;

pp. 261–262, second paragraph. *Replace item (2) with:*

(2) the name, whereabouts, and present condition of the individual beneficiary, including a letter from the beneficiary's attending physician detailing the illness or injury;

p. 262. *Replace first full paragraph with:*

An organization exempt from registration that makes a material change in its legal status, officers, address, or similar changes must, within 30 days, file a report informing the division of its current legal status, business address, business telephone, officers, and primary contact person.

The division may by rule require organizations exempt from registration to file a notice of claim of exemption, prescribe the contents of the notice of claim, and require a filing fee for the notice.

## Other Requirements

*Contracts.*

p. 262. *Replace subsection with:*

*Contracts.* A charitable organization may only engage the services of a professional fund-raiser or professional solicitor through a written agreement. Likewise, these persons may not provide services to a charitable organization in the absence of a written agreement.

## Unique Provisions

### *Disclosures.*

p. 262. *Replace subsection with:*

*Disclosures.* A paid solicitor who makes a person-to-person solicitation for a charitable organization registered or required to be registered under this law (see above) must first obtain an information card from the division or the organization.

Each permit and information card issued by the division must "set forth such information as will assist any person solicited to determine the purpose for which the contribution is solicited," including (1) if it is an information card or professional solicitor permit, the identity of the person making the solicitation; (2) if the permit is for a charitable organization, the identity of the organization; (3) if it is an information card, the identity of the organization for which the contributions are solicited; (4) an official acknowledgment or seal that the permit is issued by the division or, in the case of an information card, that the card is on a form supplied by the division; (5) the statement as to no guarantee by the state as to accuracy of information (see below); (6) the expiration date of the permit or identification card; and (7) any other information that the division may prescribe by rule.

In an in-person solicitation, each holder of a permit or information card must maintain in his or her possession the permit or card and display it to any person solicited. In a solicitation by telephone, the information on the permit or card must be "distinctly and clearly repeated" as part of the solicitation.

A person who solicits contributions without compensation is not required to have an information card but must clearly inform the solicitee of the charitable organization on whose behalf the solicitation is occurring.

### *Prohibited Acts.*

p. 263. *Add at end of subsection:*

A professional fund-raiser may not knowingly plan, manage, advise, counsel, consult, or prepare material for or with respect to the solicitation in the state of a charitable contribution, whether or not the organization involved is registered, unless the fund-raiser is registered with the division.

A professional solicitor may not knowingly solicit, request, promote, advertise, or sponsor the solicitation in the state of a charitable contribution, whether or not the organization involved is registered, unless the solicitor is registered with the division.

*Other.*

p. 263. *Insert as second paragraph of subsection:*

By issuing a permit or by providing forms for an information card (see above), the state does not guarantee the accuracy of any representation contained in the permit or card, nor does it warrant that any statement made by the holder of the permit or card is truthful. A statement to this effect must appear on each permit and identification card in upper-case letters. The state does not make any certification as to the "charitable worthiness" of any organization on whose behalf a solicitation is made nor as to the "moral character" of the holder of the permit or card.

## Sanctions

pp. 263–264. *Replace subsection with:*

The division may deny, suspend, or revoke an application, registration, permit, or information card, upon a finding that (1) the action is in the "public interest"; (2) the application for registration or renewal is incomplete or misleading in any material respect; (3) the applicant or registrant, or any director, officer, agent, or employee of it, has (a) violated this law; (b) been enjoined by a court, or is the subject of an administrative order issued in this or another state, if the injunction or order includes a finding or admission of fraud, breach of fiduciary duty, material misrepresentation, or if the injunction or order was based on a finding of "lack of integrity, truthfulness, or mental competence" of the applicant; (c) been convicted of a crime involving moral turpitude; (d) obtained or attempted to obtain a registration or a permit by misrepresentation; (e) materially misrepresented or caused to be misrepresented the purpose and manner in which contributed funds and property will be used in connection with any solicitation; (f) caused or allowed any paid solicitor to violate a rule made or order issued under this law by the division; (g) failed reasonably to supervise his or her agents, employees, paid solicitors, or, in the case of an organization, its professional fund-raisers or professional solicitors; (h) used or attempted to use a name that either is deceptively similar to a name used by an existing registered or exempt charitable organization or appears reasonably likely to cause confusion of names; (i) failed to timely file with the division a report required by this law or rules issued pursuant to it; or (j) failed to pay a fine imposed by the division; (4) a professional fund-raiser or professional solicitor does not have the required bond or letter of credit (see above) in force; or (5) the applicant for registration or renewal "has no charitable purpose."

The division may issue an order to revoke or suspend a claim of exemption from registration upon a finding that (1) the order is in the "public interest" and (2)(a) the notice of claim of exemption is incomplete or false or misleading in any material respect or (b) any provision of this law, or rule made or order issued by the division under this law, has been violated in connection with a charitable solicitation by any exempt organization.

The registration of any organization that fails to timely file a report or copy of a federal annual information return (see above), or files an incomplete report or return, is automatically suspended pending a final order of the division. This registration may be reinstated once the division receives the accurate report or return, an application for renewed registration, and the payment of a penalty.

As to an appeal for an individual (see above), if the organizer fails to timely file the requisite notice, a cease-and-desist order may be issued against the organizer. Such an order may also be issued when the division has reasonable cause to believe that the organizer is perpetrating a fraud against the public or in any other way intends to profit from harming the public through a charitable campaign.

An organization failing to file a registration application or renewal by the due date or filing an incomplete registration application or renewal must pay a fee (in addition to the registration fee) for each month or part of a month after the date on which the registration application or renewal were due to be filed.

A person violating this law, either by failing to comply with a requirement or by doing an act prohibited in the law, is guilty of a misdemeanor.

A person damaged as a result of a charitable solicitation can maintain a civil action for damages or injunctive relief.

The division may maintain an action for damages or injunctive relief on behalf of itself or any other person, to enforce compliance with this law.

# CHAPTER FOUR

# The State Charitable Solicitation Acts: A Comparative Analysis

p. 295, line 1. *Replace "35" with "36".*

p. 295, n. 2, line 2. *Replace "three" with "two".*

## § 4.1 DEFINITIONS

### (a) Charitable

p. 297, first full paragraph. *In line 7, replace "11" with "12".*

p. 297, n. 16, line 1. *Insert before existing text:*
Alabama (registration only),

p. 298. *Insert following item 7:*

7A. "(i) any benevolent, educational, humane, scientific, patriotic, social welfare or advocacy, public health, environmental, conservation, civic, or philanthropic objective, or (ii) an objective to benefit law enforcement officers, firefighters or other persons who protect the public safety."[26.1]

p. 299. *Replace item 23 with:*

23. Any purpose "described in Section 501(c)(3) of the Internal Revenue Code" or "[a]ny voluntary health and welfare, charitable, benevolent, philanthropic, patriotic, educational, humane, scientific, public health, environmental conservation, civic, or other eleemosynary purpose or for the benefit of law enforcement personnel, fire fighters, or other public safety organizations."[42]

p. 301. *Replace item 41 with:*

41. "[A]ny benevolent, educational, philanthropic, humane, patriotic, religious, eleemosynary, social welfare or advocacy, public health, environmental, conservation, civic, or other charitable objective or for the benefit of a public safety, law enforcement, or firefighter fraternal association."[60]

### (e) Contribution

p. 305. *Insert at end of subsection:*

The amount or value of a charitable contribution may be pertinent in the application of a provision of a state's charitable solicitation act. For example, certain "small" solicitations are often exempted from these acts; these determinations are made on the basis of the monetary value of the aggregate

[26.1] Delaware.

gifts.[87.1] In most instances, these calculations are made on the basis of the value of the payments that are in fact contributions. However, in the only provision of its type, the law in one state is that "[r]eference to the dollar amount of 'contributions' in this article means in the case of promises to pay, or payments for merchandise or rights of any other description, the value of the total amount promised to be paid for the merchandise or rights and not merely that portion of the purchase price to be applied to a charitable purpose."[87.2]

## (g)  Professional Fund-Raiser

p. 305, last line. *Replace "29" with "28".*

p. 305, n. 91. *Delete "Mississippi,".*

p. 306, line 15. *Replace "nine" with "eight".*

p. 306, n. 97. *Delete "Mississippi,".*

p. 306, line 17. *Replace "eight" with "nine".*

p. 306, n. 99, line 1. *Insert "Mississippi," following fourth comma.*

p. 306, third paragraph. *Insert as last sentence:*

In still another state, the term used is professional fund-raising counsel or consultant.[104.1]

p. 307, first full paragraph. *In first line, replace "three" with "four".*

p. 307, n. 110. *Insert before existing material:*

Delaware,

## (h)  Professional Solicitor

p. 308, line 1. *Replace "34" with "35".*

---

[87.1] See *infra* §  4.4(i).
[87.2] Alabama.
[104.1] Utah.

p. 308, n. 118, line 1. *Insert following second comma:*
Delaware,

p. 308, line 2. *Replace "17" with "18".*

p. 308, n. 119, line 1. *Insert before existing material:*
Delaware,

p. 308, fourth full paragraph. *In first line, replace "four" with "five".*

p. 308, n. 129. *Insert before existing material:*
Alabama,

### (i)   Commercial Co-Venturer

p. 309, second paragraph of subsection. *In last line, replace "six" with "seven".*

p. 309, n. 139. *Insert before existing material:*
Alabama,

### (j)   Administrative Agency

p. 310, line 3. *Replace "21" with "22".*

p. 310, n. 145, line 1. *Insert following fourth comma:*
Delaware,

## § 4.2   PREAPPROVAL

p. 311, first paragraph of section. *Replace second sentence with:*

This permission, which must be secured by both domestic (in-state) and foreign (out-of-state) charitable organizations, is characterized as a registration in 30 states,[164] an application for a license in 3 states,[165] a filing of a statement in 2 states,[166] a filing for a certificate in 1 state,[167] and a filing of a solicitation notice in 1 state.[168]

p. 311, n. 164, line 1. *Insert before existing material:*
Alabama,

p. 311, n. 164, line 4. *Insert following second comma:*
Utah,

p. 311, n. 166. *Delete "and Hawaii".*

p. 311. *Delete n. 168.*

p. 311, first paragraph of section. *In line 11, replace "Nine" with "Eight".*

p. 311, n. 171. *Delete "Alabama,".*

p. 314, line 6. *Replace "18" with "19".*

p. 314, n. 180, line 1. *Insert before existing material:*
Alabama,

p. 314, n. 180, line 1. *Delete "Hawaii,".*

p. 314, n. 180, line 3. *Insert following second comma:*
Tennessee,

p. 314, line 12. *Replace "21" with "20".*

p. 314, n. 182, line 1. *Delete "Hawaii,".*

p. 314, line 20. *Replace "12" with "13".*

p. 314, n. 183, line 1. *Insert before existing material:*
Alabama,

\* p. 314. *Add at end of subsection:*

The burdens of registration imposed on charitable organizations engaging in multistate charitable solicitations appear to be lessening, as the consequence of development of a unified registration statement. More than 30 states and the District of Columbia have agreed to utilize the form. At this time, six states require supplemental information. This form is optional for use by participating charities.[185.1]


## § 4.3 ANNUAL REPORTING

p. 315, line 4. *Replace "24" with "25".*

p. 315, n. 187, line 1. *Insert before existing material:*
Alabama,

p. 315, line 8. *Replace "Nine" with "Eight".*

p. 315, n. 193. *Delete "Alabama,".*

p. 316, second full paragraph, line 5. *Replace "four" with "five".*

p. 316, n. 200. *Insert before existing material:*
Alabama,

p. 316, second full paragraph, line 6. *Replace "nine" with "ten".*

p. 316, n. 202, line 1. *Insert following last comma:*
Tennessee,

p. 316, third full paragraph, line 3. *Replace "five" with "six".*

p. 316, n. 205. *Delete "and"; insert before period:*
", and Utah"

p. 316. *Insert at end of section:*

In two states, a charitable organization soliciting contributions in the state must file financial reports on a quarterly basis during its first year of existence.[207.1]

---

\*  [185.1] This unified registration statement and its instructions are reproduced as Appendix J. Not included in this appendix are the supplementary forms that must be filed in connection with registrations in the states of Arkansas, Georgia, Maine, Mississippi, North Dakota, and Tennessee.
[207.1] Tennessee and Utah.

## § 4.4 EXEMPTIONS

### (a) Churches

p. 317, n. 209. *Replace "220-229" with "§ 8.3".*

### (b) Other Religious Organizations

p. 318, line 1. *Replace "Twenty-five" with "Twenty-four".*

p. 318, n. 213, line 1. *Delete "Hawaii,".*

p. 318. *Delete n. 214.*

p. 318, n. 215, line 1. *Insert before existing material:*
Alabama,

p. 318, n. 215, line 1. *Delete "Hawaii,".*

### (c) Educational Institutions

p. 318, first paragraph. *Delete second sentence.*

p. 318, n. 217, line 1. *Insert before existing material:*
Alabama,

p. 318, n. 217, line 1. *Delete "Hawaii,".*

p. 318, second paragraph of subsection. *In first line, replace "Ten" with "Nine".*

p. 318, n. 218, line 1. *Delete "Hawaii,".*

p. 319, n. 221. *Replace, in both instances, "at 368" with "§ 11.3(b)(v)"; replace "387-402" with "§ 11.3(b)(i)-(iv)".*

p. 319, n. 222, line 1. *Insert before existing material:*

Alabama,

p. 319, n. 222, line 1. *Delete "Hawaii,".*

p. 319, second paragraph. *Replace third sentence with:*

Six states exempt, from the registration requirements, "parent-teacher associations" affiliated with an educational institution,[223] six states so exempt alumni organizations;[224] three states so exempt student groups;[225] and one state so exempts a broadcast medium owned or operated by an educational institution.[225.1]

## (d)  Libraries

p. 319, first paragraph of subsection. *In first line, replace "Eight" with "Seven".*

## (f)  Health Care Institutions

p. 320, first paragraph. *In line 1, replace "Ten" with "Nine".*

p. 320, n. 231. *In line 1, delete "Hawaii,".*

p. 320, first paragraph. *Insert as last sentence:*

One state similarly exempts health care foundations but not hospitals as such.[232.1]

---

[223] Arkansas, Connecticut, Kentucky, Pennsylvania, and Utah.

[224] Alabama, Illinois, Connecticut, Kentucky, Pennsylvania, and Rhode Island.

[225] Kentucky, Maine, and Utah.

[225.1] Utah.

[232.1] Alabama.

### (g) Other Health Care Provider Organizations

p. 320, first paragraph of subsection. *In first line, replace "Six" with "Seven".*

p. 320, n. 235. *Insert before existing material:*
Alabama (where no paid fund-raising),

p. 320, n. 235. *Insert before existing material:*
Alabama (where no paid fund-raising),

p. 320, first paragraph of subsection. *In second line, replace "Five" with "Six".*

p. 320, n. 236. *Insert before existing material:*
Alabama (where no paid fund-raising),

### (h) Membership Organizations

p. 321, line 1. *Insert "prospective" before "donor's".*

p. 321, first complete paragraph. *Delete second sentence.*

p. 321, n. 245, line 1. *Insert before existing material:*
Alabama,

p. 321, n. 245, line 1. *Delete "Hawaii,".*

p. 321. *Delete n. 246.*

p. 321, n. 249. *Replace "Hawaii" with "Alabama".*

p. 321, n. 250, line 1. *Insert before existing material:*
Alabama,

### (i) Small Solicitations

p. 321, second paragraph of subsection. *In line 6, replace "eight" with "nine".*

p. 321, n. 252. *Insert before existing material:*
Alabama,

p. 322, line 2. *Replace "states" with "state".*

p. 322, n. 256. *Replace "Hawaii" with "Mississippi".*

### (j)  Solicitations for Specified Individuals

p. 322, n. 265, line 1. *Insert before existing material:*
Alabama,

p. 322. n. 265, line 1. *Delete "Hawaii,".*

p. 322, n. 265, line 2. *Insert "(but only where the individual has sustained a life-threatening illness or injury)" after "Utah".*

### (k)  Political Organizations

p. 323, line 2 of subsection. *Replace "Five" with "Six".*

p. 323, n. 270. *Insert before existing material:*
Alabama,

### (l)  Veterans' Organizations

p. 323, line 1 of subsection. *Replace "Nine" with "Ten".*

p. 323, n. 272, line 1. *Insert before existing material:*
Alabama,

### (n)  Other Categories of Exempted Organizations

p. 324, line 7. *Replace "ten" with "twelve".*

p. 324, n. 282, line 1. *Insert before existing material:*
Alabama

p. 324, n. 282, line 2. *Insert following third comma:*
Utah

p. 324, line 8. *Replace "seven" with "eight".*

p. 324, n. 283. *Insert before existing material:*
Alabama

p. 324, line 8. *Replace "six" with "seven".*

p. 324, n. 284. *Insert before existing material:*
Alabama

p. 324, line 9. *Replace first "five" with "six".*

p. 324, n. 285. *Insert before existing material:*
Alabama

p. 324, line 9. *Replace second "five" with "six".*

p. 324, n. 286. *Insert before existing material:*
Alabama

p. 324, line 9. *Replace "four" with "five".*

p. 324, n. 287. *Insert before existing material:*
Alabama

p. 324, line 12. *Replace "four" with "five".*

p. 324, n. 289. *Insert before existing material:*
Alabama

p. 324, lines 14 and 15. *Replace "two states" with "one state".*

p. 324, n. 293. *Delete "Utah and".*

p. 324, line 15. *Insert following second semicolon:*

civil defense organizations in two states;[294.1]

p. 324, line 18. *Insert following semicolon:*

civil rights organizations in one state;[298.1] fraternities and sororities associated with a variety of organizations in one state;[298.2]

p. 325. *Replace last sentence of carryover paragraph with:*

In one state, there is an exemption from registration and reporting for state-based charitable trusts[306] and in another state this type of an exemption for debt counseling agencies.[307]

p. 325. *Replace note 306 with:*

[306] Ohio.

p. 325. *Replace note 307 with:*

[307] Virginia.

p. 325. *Delete notes 308 and 309.*

pp. 325–326, last paragraph. *Delete second sentence and note 315.*

## § 4.5  REGULATION OF PROFESSIONAL FUND-RAISERS

p. 326, first paragraph of section. *In line 4, replace "34" with "35".*

p. 326, n. 318, line 1. *Insert before existing material:*

Alabama,

p. 326, fourth paragraph of section. *In line 3, replace "27" with "28".*

p. 326, n. 321, line 1. *Insert before existing material:*

Alabama,

---

[294.1] Tennessee (total exemption) and Utah.
[298.1] Alabama.
[298.2] *Id.*

p. 327, n. 322. *Insert "(or a letter of credit in that amount)" before third comma.*

p. 327, line 4. *Replace "seven" with "eight".*

p. 327, n. 325. *Insert before existing material:*
Alabama,

p. 327, n. 328. *Insert as second sentence:*
Subsequently, the state of Utah enacted a rule allowing the use of a letter of credit in lieu of a bond.

## § 4.6   REGULATION OF PROFESSIONAL SOLICITORS

p. 327, first paragraph of section. *In line 6, replace "29" with "30".*

p. 327, n. 331, line 1. *Insert before existing material:*
Alabama,

p. 328, n. 333. *Insert "(or a letter of credit in that amount)" following second comma.*

## § 4.7   REGULATION OF COMMERCIAL CO-VENTURERS

p. 328, first paragraph of section. *In line 1, replace "Seventeen" with "Eighteen".*

p. 328, n. 339, line 1. *Insert before existing material:*
Alabama,

p. 328, n. 340. *Insert before existing material:*
Alabama,

p. 328, n. 341. *Insert before existing material:*
Alabama,

p. 328, second paragraph of section. *In line 1, replace "two" with "three".*

p. 328, n. 344. *Insert before existing material:*
Alabama,

## § 4.9 AVAILABILITY OF RECORDS

p. 332, line 4. *Replace "38" with "40".*

p. 332, n. 372, line 1. *Insert before existing material:*
Alabama,

p. 332, n. 372, line 1. *Insert after "Connecticut,":*
Delaware,

p. 332, line 6. *Replace "six" with "seven".*

p. 332, n. 373. *Insert following first comma:*
Delaware,

## § 4.10 CONTRACTS

p. 332, second paragraph of section. *In line 2, replace "25" with "26".*

p. 332, n. 374, line 1. *Insert before existing material:*
Alabama,

p. 332, second paragraph of section. *In line 3, replace "26" with "29".*

p. 332, n. 375, line 1. *Insert before existing material:*
Alabama,

p. 332, n. 375, line 1. *Insert following second comma:*
Delaware

p. 332, n. 375, line 4. *Insert following second comma:*
Utah,

## § 4.14 DISCLOSURE STATEMENTS AND LEGENDS

p. 332, second paragraph of section, line 3. *Replace "five" with "Six".*

p. 332, n. 376. *Insert before existing material:*
Alabama,


## § 4.11 REGISTERED AGENT REQUIREMENTS

p. 333, third paragraph of section. *In line 5, replace "19" with "20".*

p. 334, n. 381, line 1. *Insert before existing material:*
Alabama,


## § 4.12 PROHIBITED ACTS

p. 334, first paragraph of section. *In line 4, replace "43" with "44".*

p. 334, n. 382, line 1. *Insert following "Connecticut,":*
Delaware,


## § 4.14 DISCLOSURE STATEMENTS AND LEGENDS

p. 336, second paragraph of section. *In line 6, replace "seven" with "eight".*

p. 336, third paragraph of section, line 1. *Replace "Ten" with "Eleven".*

p. 336, n. 399. *Insert following fourth comma:*
Utah (obligation of professional solicitor),

p. 336, n. 400, line 1. *Insert "Mississippi," following third comma.*

## § 4.17 FIDUCIARY RELATIONSHIPS

p. 339, second line of section. *Replace "six" with "seven".*

p. 339, n. 411. *Insert "Mississippi," following second comma.*

## § 4.19 MISCELLANEOUS PROVISIONS

p. 340, first line of section. *Replace "15" with "16".*

p. 340, n. 417, line 1. *Insert "Mississippi," following seventh comma.*

p. 340, second line of section. *Replace "13" with "14".*

p. 340, n. 418, line 1. *Insert "Mississippi," following sixth comma.*

p. 341, line 1. *Replace "30" with "31".*

p. 341, n. 423, line 1. *Insert before existing material:*
Alabama,

p. 341, fourth paragraph, line 4. *Replace "five" with "four".*

p. 341, n. 428, line 1. *Delete "Hawaii (publication of information in a newspaper),".*

p. 341, sixth paragraph, line 3. *Replace "another" with "two states".*

p. 341, sixth paragraph, lines 3–4. *Replace "the latter jurisdiction" with "one of these jurisdictions".*

p. 341, sixth paragraph, line 6. *Insert footnote at end of line:*

431.1 Washington.

p. 341, sixth paragraph. *Insert following existing material:*
In a third jurisdiction, telephone solicitation for a charitable gift by a professional fund-raiser or professional solicitor must be confined to the hours be-

tween 9:00 A.M. and 9:00 P.M.[431.2] In this jurisdiction, telephone calls for charitable solicitation purposes may not be made on Sunday.

p. 341, n. 431. *Insert before existing material:*

Delaware and

## § 4.20 SANCTIONS

p. 341, last text line. *Replace "27" with "28".*

p. 342, n. 432, line 1. *Insert before existing material:*

Alabama,

p. 342, line 3. *Replace "31" with "32".*

p. 342, n. 435, line 1. *Insert before existing material:*

Alabama,

p. 342, line 8. *Replace "eight" with "nine".*

p. 342, n. 438. *Insert following second comma:*

Delaware,

p. 342. *Insert after carryover paragraph:*

In two states, there is a monetary penalty for failure to timely file a complete financial report during the charitable organization's first year of registration.[438.1] In one state, a cease-and-desist order may, under certain circumstances, be issued against an organizer of a solicitation for a specified individual.[438.2]

---

[431.2] Mississippi.
[438.1] Tennessee and Utah.
[438.2] Utah.

## § 4.21 OTHER LAWS

p. 343, n. 441. *Insert at end:*

Clearly, a charitable organization organized in one state and maintaining an office or similar physical presence in another state is doing business in the latter state. The general rule is that merely mailing charitable solicitation material into a state is not doing business in that state, although a contrary approach can be established by statute or regulation. In many states, the determination as to whether an organization is doing business in a state is under the jurisdiction of the secretary of state, whereas the registration and reporting requirements of a charitable solicitation act are administered by the attorney general. In some states (such as California), a determination that a charitable organization is doing business in the state leads to a requirement that the organization file for and receive a ruling as to its tax-exempt status in the state (or else be subject to state taxation). Thus, fund-raising in a state can entail an obligation on the part of the charitable organization to file with three separate agencies in the state.

p. 343. *Insert footnote at end of item 3:*

442.1 E.g., Horner and Makens, "Securities Regulation of Fundraising Activities of Religious and Other Nonprofit Organizations," XXVII *Stetson L. Rev.* (No. 2) 473 (Fall 1997).

\* p. 343, n. 443. *Insert as second paragraph:*

The state of Minnesota, in mid-1999, charged a charity located in Louisiana and its fund-raising company with the use of deceptive tactics in raising money, by telephone, for terminally ill children (Williams, "Minn. Sues Charity, Solicitors Over Telephone Appeals," XI *Chron. of Phil.* (No. 14) 29 (May 6, 1999)).

\* p. 343, n. 443. *Insert following existing material:*

A challenge to a state's use of an unfair trade practices act and state sweepstakes law to regulate charitable fund-raising failed, with the court finding that the plaintiffs lacked standing to bring the suit (*American Charities for Reasonable Fundraising Regulation, Inc. v. Shiffrin*, 46 F. Supp. 2d 143 (D. Conn. 1999)).

p. 343. *Insert footnote at end of item 6:*

444 In addition to these state requirements, there are hundreds of county and city ordinances, as noted *supra* note 1. The constitutionality of these ordinances is a subject that is attracting increasing attention. Two of these ordinances, portions of which were struck down as being unconstitutional, are discussed in Chapter 5 (see the analyses of the *Gospel Missions of America* case).

\*    One of the obvious aspects of these ordinances is the enormous administrative and financial burden they place on charities that raise funds statewide, regionally, and certainly nationally. A court has, however, rejected the argument that the costs of compliance with these ordinances is an unconstitutional form of direct or indirect regulation of interstate commerce; it also held that the substantial benefit to the county involved outweighs any compliance difficulties. Further, a free speech argument (see *infra* § 5.3) failed; the court myopically wrote: "The County also correctly points out that localities are well within their power to regulate charitable solicitation within their territorial boundaries" (*American Charities for Reasonable Fundraising Regulation, Inc.* v. *Pinellas County*, 32 F. Supp. 2d 1308, 1325 (M.D. Fla. 1998)).

# State Regulation of Fund-Raising: Legal Issues

## § 5.2  THE POLICE POWER

p. 364. *Insert footnote at end of first paragraph:*

[30.1] The Supreme Court ruled that a state having a property tax exemption for charitable organizations cannot deny that exemption to charitable entities solely because they principally serve nonresidents. The Court reasoned that this type of discriminatory tax exemption is a violation of the commerce clause and thus cannot stand, notwithstanding the states' general authority to legislate on subjects relating to the health, life, and safety of their citizens (*Camps Newfound/Owatonna, Inc.* v. *Town of Harrison, Maine,* 117 S. Ct. 1590 (1997)). In general, Brody, "Hocking the Halo: Implications of the Charities' Winning Briefs in *Camps Newfound/Owatonna, Inc.*," XXVII *Stetson L. Rev.* (No. 2) 433 (Fall 1997).

p. 364, n. 31. *Insert at end:*

Likewise, *Gospel Missions of America* v. *Bennett,* 951 F. Supp. 1429 (C.D. Fla. 1997) (court found that it was constitutional for a city ordinance to require charity to supply an "information card" before soliciting charitable contributions, mandate disclosure of information relating solely to the solicitation, require that a system of accounting be maintained according to customary accounting principles, and authorize the city to investigate the books and records underlying charitable organizations' financial statements; comparable provisions in a county ordinance were also upheld).

\* p. 366. *Insert following second full quotation:*

As noted, counties, cities, and like jurisdictions also possess the police power. One court broadly stated that "localities are well within their power to regulate charitable solicitation within their territorial boundaries."[42.1] These ordinances may be authorized by state statute and often permit the governmental jurisdiction to enact rules that are more stringent than those imposed by state law.

p. 366. *Insert footnote at end of last full paragraph:*

[43.1] However, once that burden is met, these laws can be a fertile field for the finding of constitutional law violations (e.g., *Gospel Missions of America* v. *Bennett, supra* note 31).

\* p. 367, n. 47. *Replace "5.10" with "5.11".*

## § 5.3 FUND-RAISING AS FREE SPEECH

### (b) Free Speech Principles in Fund-Raising Context

p. 381, n. 124. *Insert following existing material:*

A brief history of the caselaw in this area is the subject of Copilevitz, "The Historical Role of the First Amendment in Charitable Appeals," XXVII *Stetson L. Rev.* (No. 2) 457 (Fall 1997).

### (c) State of Law Subsequent to Supreme Court Decisions

p. 385. *Insert after second full paragraph:*

A challenge to a city ordinance regulating charitable fund-raising was unsuccessful, with a federal appellate court holding that the regulatory framework was constitutional.[151.1] However, the ordinance had been amended just before the court's consideration of the case; the regulatory scheme was substantially simplified and various provisions excised that would have been rendered unconstitutional as being in violation of free speech rights.[151.2] One of the provisions that was timely removed accorded the government the authority

---

[42.1] *American Charities for Reasonable Fundraising Regulation, Inc.* v. *Pinellas County,* 32 F. Supp. 2d 1308, 1325 (M.D. Fla. 1998).

[151.1] *International Society for Krishna Consciousness of Houston, Inc.* v. *City of Houston, supra* note 2.

[151.2] *Id.* at 546–47.

to disqualify an applicant charitable organization when more than 25 percent of the funds to be collected were to be used for noncharitable purposes.

p. 386, n. 160, second paragraph. *Delete first sentence.*

p. 388. *Insert after first full paragraph:*

A section of a county[178.1] ordinance regulating charitable solicitations was found unconstitutional because it enabled the agency involved to deny or revoke a required information card if the agency found that the percentage of contributions raised that would be available for charitable programs is "unreasonably small," based on various criteria including "inefficient operation" or the payment of unreasonable compensation. The court observed that although the provision did not constitute a "fixed percentage limitation" on the costs of solicitation, it nonetheless imposed an unwarranted "cost-effectiveness" requirement.[178.2] This provision, said the court, "impermissibly conditions the exercise of First Amendment rights on business efficiency," including allowing the government to arbitrarily determine the value of services.[178.3]

p. 389. *Insert following carryover paragraph:*

Another aspect of the interrelationship between the principles of free speech and charitable fund-raising involves burgeoning disclosure requirements.[179.1] One court stated that the "potential chilling effect [of certain disclosure requirements] on the exercise of [protected] First Amendment rights . . . is manifest, together with the invasion of privacy."[179.2] One court struck down two provisions of a city[179.3] ordinance on this basis: one that required a "detailed financial statement" for the most recent year and one that required disclosure of the name, address, and telephone number of each trustee, director, and officer. These disclosures were said to "directly expose the applicant's internal operations to public scrutiny and are unrelated to any legitimate governmental interest, including the [c]ity's stated interest in preventing fraudulent solicitations."[179.4]

---

[178.1] Los Angeles.

[178.2] *Gospel Missions of America v. Bennett, supra* note 31, at 1451.

[178.3] *Id.*

[179.1] See, e.g., §§ 4.14 and 4.16. The recent emphasis on forms of disclosure requirements by governments is a response to the fact that they can no longer regulate fund-raising on the basis of percentages of funds devoted to program or to solicitation costs.

[179.2] *Holy Spirit Association for Unification of World Christianity v. Hodge, supra* note 160, at 601.

[179.3] Los Angeles.

[179.4] *Gospel Missions of America v. Bennett, supra* note 31, at 1443.

On this basis, this court struck down two provisions of a county[179.5] ordinance. One, part of a registration requirement, mandated that applicants file a "specific statement of all contributions collected or received" within the year preceding the filing, including the "expenditures or use made of such contributions, together with the names and addresses of all persons or associations receiving . . . compensation . . . from such contributions and the respective amounts thereof." This law was deemed facially invalid because it is "unduly burdensome, unnecessarily compels applicants to disclose their internal operations, and fails to materially advance the [c]ounty's substantial and legitimate interest in preventing fraudulent solicitations."[179.6] The other required disclosure of the names and addresses of an applicant's directors and officers, and submission of a copy of the applicant's board resolution authorizing the solicitation. Said the court: "These requirements similarly chill the exercise of free speech rights by compelling publication of the applicant's private and internal operations and are not intimately related to the [c]ounty's legitimate interest in preventing fraud."[179.7]

It is nonetheless clear that the basic features of a state's charitable solicitation act will pass constitutional law muster. This was illustrated by a federal court decision in 1998, upholding one of these laws[179.8]—principally against a free speech challenge. The features of this law that were found to be lawful are the registration and disclosure requirements, the registration fee, a bond or letter of credit requirement, and the authority in the state to deny or revoke a fund-raising license in certain circumstances.[179.9]

\* Likewise, a county charitable solicitation ordinance[179.10] was upheld in the face of a broad challenge, including one based on free speech principles. The ordinance contains a typical array of registration, reporting, and disclosure requirements, imposed on charitable organizations and professional solicitors. The court observed that the purpose of the ordinance, which is to prevent fraud and other forms of deception in charitable solicitations, amounted to a substantial county

---

[179.5] Los Angeles.

[179.6] *Gospel Missions of America* v. *Bennett, supra* note 31, at 1450.

[179.7] *Id.*

[179.8] The Utah Charitable Solicitations Act.

[179.9] *American Target Advertising, Inc.* v. *Giani,* 23 F. Supp. 2d 1303 (D. Utah 1998). Registration fees and a bond requirement were upheld in *Dayton Area Visually Impaired Persons, Inc.* v. *Fisher,* 70 F.3d 1474 (6th Cir. 1995).

\* A provision in a state's constitution, barring advertising of bingo games by charitable (and certain other nonprofit) organizations, was struck down by a federal district court as being a violation of commercial speech guaranteed under the First Amendment. The advertising restrictions were found to be unnecessarily extensive and the state was found to have available other, nonspeech restrictions that would adequately protect its interests. This case was ruled not to involve the higher level of free speech associated with charitable fund-raising (see *supra* § 5.3(b)(iv)) (*Association of Charitable Games of Missouri* v. *Missouri Gaming Commission,* 1998 U.S. Dist. LEXIS 14433 (W.D. Mo. 1998)).

\* [179.10] An ordinance of Pinellas County, Florida.

interest. The court found that the various provisions of the ordinance that were challenged are sufficiently narrowly tailored to satisfy First Amendment scrutiny.[179.11]

## § 5.4   DUE PROCESS RIGHTS

p. 398, second full paragraph. *Replace last sentence with:*

This type of rule is unconstitutional inasmuch as there is an absence of procedural and substantive criteria for making that determination.[239.1] In a comparable setting, this type of law was struck down because of the lack of appropriate procedural safeguards, because there were no time limits within which the government had to act.[239.2]

p. 398. *Insert after second full paragraph:*

Still another illustration: City and county[239.3] ordinances were found to be facially invalid because, having mandated the use of an "information card," the governments were authorized to void the card on the basis of information received by the governments and there were no time constraints as to issuance of a replacement card.[239.4] Another provision of the county ordinance was invalidated because it required the charitable organization to return the solicitation card following the close of a solicitation, with no opportunity to obtain an extension of the solicitation period.

p. 398. *Insert footnote at end of section:*

[242.1] In general, *Fernandes v. Limmer,* 663 F.2d 619 (5th Cir. 1981), cert. dismissed, 458 U.S. 1124 (1982).

## *   § 5.5   EQUAL PROTECTION RIGHTS

p. 402, n. 267. *Insert following existing material:*

In a case involving the principles of commercial speech, a court found an equal protection violation, in that a provision in a state's constitution precluded charitable organizations from advertising their

---

* [179.11] *American Charities for Reasonable Fundraising Regulation, Inc. v. Pinellas County, supra* note 42.1.

[239.1] Rules of this nature are also unconstitutional because of the discretion vested in government officials (see § 5.6) and because of vagueness (see § 5.7A).

[239.2] *Gospel Missions of America v. Bennett, supra* note 31.

[239.3] Los Angeles.

[239.4] *Gospel Missions of America v. Bennett, supra* note 31.

bingo games, while riverboat casinos in the state were not prohibited from advertising casino gambling. (*Association of Charitable Games of Missouri* v. *Missouri Gaming Commission, supra* note 179.9)

## § 5.6 DELEGATION OF LEGISLATIVE AUTHORITY

p. 402. *Insert after second full paragraph of section:*

Thus, the Supreme Court observed that a "narrowly drawn ordinance, that does not vest in [governmental] officials the undefined power to determine what messages residents will hear may serve [the government's] important interests without running afoul of the First Amendment."[267.1] However, "[i]n the area of free expression, a licensing statute placing unbridled discretion in the hands of a government official or agency constitutes a prior restraint and may result in censorship."[267.2]

p. 404. *Insert following second full paragraph:*

Portions of a city[276.1] ordinance regulating charitable solicitations were found unconstitutional because the provisions involved improperly placed "unbridled discretion" in the hands of city officials, "constituting a prior restraint on protected speech lacking procedural safeguards to guard against potential censorship."[276.2] One of these provisions accorded the department that regulates charitable fund-raising the power to make a "judgment" as to whether a charitable organization's registration statement disclosed "sufficient information" to the public; that agency was empowered to seek additional information if it wished. Another defective provision, as part of the ability of the department to issue information cards in connection with a charitable solicitation, empowered the agency to include "any additional information which in the opinion of the [d]epartment will be of assistance to the public in determining the nature and worthiness of the solicitation." Still another provision found constitutionally infirm was a requirement that the department verify that an applicant professional fund-raiser is of "good character." In addition, the ordinance failed constitutional law muster on this ground because the applicant charity must demonstrate "sufficient financial resources" to "successfully fulfill" its obligations; certain procedures in the law were deemed to be utter failures in obviating the dangers of a censorship system.

[267.1] *Hynes* v. *Mayor of Oradell, supra* note 56, at 617.

[267.2] *City of Lakewood* v. *Plain Dealer Publishing Co.*, 486 U.S. 750, 757 (1988).

[276.1] Los Angeles.

[276.2] *Gospel Missions of America* v. *Bennett, supra* note 31, at 1443.

Provisions of a county[276.3] ordinance regulating charitable fund-raising were found unconstitutional for the same reason: unbridled discretion in governmental officials. One provision found facially invalid enabled the governing commission, when "in its opinion" the application for an information card did not disclose "sufficient information," to require the applicant to file "such additional information as the commission may require." The information card may be denied or revoked if the commission determines that the applicant is "unfit to be trusted . . . or has a bad moral character, intemperate habits, or a bad reputation for truth, honesty, or integrity"; that provision was held "blatantly unconstitutional."[276.4] Still another defective provision enabled the commission to deny or revoke an information card if it found that the percentage of contributions raised for charitable activities is "unreasonably small" because of "inefficient operation, the payment of one or more salaries in amounts substantially greater than the reasonable value of the services performed, or for other similar reasons."[276.5]

## § 5.7   TREATMENT OF RELIGIOUS ORGANIZATIONS

### (a)   Basic Concepts

p. 406. *Insert after second full paragraph:*

Subsequently, the Supreme Court further articulated the applicable law on this point:

> It is part of our settled jurisprudence that "the Establishment Clause prohibits government from abandoning secular purposes in order to put an imprimatur on one religion, or on religion as such, or to favor the adherents of any sect or religious organization." The core notion animating the requirement that a statute possess "a secular legislative purpose" and that "its principal or primary effect . . . be one that neither advances nor inhibits religion," is not only that government may not be overly hostile to religion but also that it may not place its prestige, coercive authority, or resources behind a single religious faith or behind religious belief in general, compelling nonadherents to support the practices or proselytizing of favored religious organizations

---

[276.3] Los Angeles.

[276.4] *Gospel Missions of America* v. *Bennett, supra* note 31, at 1451.

[276.5] This last provision was also deemed unconstitutional on the ground that the percentage-of-contributions concept is contrary to free speech rights (see § 5.3).

and conveying the message that those who do not contribute gladly are less than full members of the community.[296.1]

Thus, an exemption for religious organizations can provide unjustifiable assistance to religious solicitors and, in some instances, "cannot but 'convey a message of endorsement' to the slighted members of the community."[296.2]

### (b) Constitutionality of Exemption

p. 408. *Insert footnote at end of third full paragraph:*

[309.1] The rationales of this and similar opinions, however, are today to be questioned, in that they antedate the Supreme Court trilogy of cases (see § 5.7(b)).

p. 409, n. 312. *Replace "294" and substitute "293".*

p. 411. *Insert following third full paragraph:*

These principles were applied in connection with a case involving city and county[318.1] ordinances which, although they provided an exemption for solicitations made "solely for evangelical, missionary or religious purposes," authorized the government involved, when this type of solicitation was made "in a manner which, in the opinion of [the government], is calculated to give, or may give, the impression . . . that the purpose of such solicitation is either in whole or in part charitable," to investigate the matter and publicize its findings "as it deems best to advise the public of the facts of the case." These ordinances were found to be in violation of the establishment clause, in that they were in contravention of the criteria laid down by the Supreme Court in this area.[318.2] The city and county failed to articulate a secular legislative purpose that would justify their preference for solicitations solely for religious purposes. By exclusively exempting solicitations for religious purposes, the ordinances were held to be impermissibly advancing religion. The ordinances were said to create excessive entanglement between church and state by requiring the city and county governments to examine and monitor religious solicitations, to determine whether a solicitation "has been, is being or is intended to be" for religious purposes, to review the true purpose of the solicitation (in the government's opinion) and whether any element of the fund-raising is "charitable," and, depending on its findings, take certain

[296.1] *Texas Monthly, Inc.* v. *Bullock,* 489 U.S. 1, 8–9 (1989) (citations omitted).
[296.2] *Id.* at 15 (citations omitted).
[318.1] Los Angeles.
[318.2] See the text *supra* accompanied by note 312.

action. The court wrote that this "government involvement in religious activity is excessive and is a 'continuing one calling for official and continuing surveillance leading to an impermissible degree of entanglement.' "[318.3]

## § 5.7A   OTHER CONSTITUTIONAL LAW ISSUES (NEW)

Other principles of constitutional law can operate to void a charitable fundraising statute. These are usually variants of free speech considerations[333.1] but warrant special emphasis.

A statute can be unconstitutionally vague. Laws of this nature are found to be contrary to constitutional precepts when they are so vague that persons "of common intelligence must necessarily guess at [their] meaning and differ as to [their] application."[333.2] The Supreme Court stated: "The general test of vagueness applies with particular force in review of laws dealing with speech. 'Stricter standards of permissible statutory vagueness may be applied to a statute having a potentially inhibiting effect on speech; a man may the less be required to act at his peril here, because the free dissemination of ideas may be the loser.' "[333.3] One court struck down a registration requirement because the law, in addition to specifying certain information that had to be provided, also allowed the government involved to require, in its discretion, additional information (a common provision). Inasmuch as, "[f]rom reading the statute, it is impossible to discern with precision what information must be provided" as part of the registration process, the vagueness caused the law to be found facially invalid.[333.4]

A government cannot mandate or regulate the content of protected speech. This has particular relevance to the increasing tendency of states to require a soliciting charitable organization to make certain statements to prospective donors. In one instance, city and county[333.5] ordinances that required the use of an "information card" were held unconstitutional because the ordinances mandated the inclusion of information which the city and county viewed as being of "assistance to the public in determining the nature and worthiness of the solicitation."[333.6]

---

[318.3] *Gospel Missions of America* v. *Bennett, supra* note 31, at 1449, 1452 (citation omitted).

[333.1] In general, see § 5.3.

[333.2] *Connally* v. *General Construction Co.,* 269 U.S. 385, 391 (1926).

[333.3] *Hynes* v. *Mayor of Oradell, supra* note 56, at 620 (quoting *Smith* v. *California,* 361 U.S. 147, 151 (1959)).

[333.4] *Gospel Missions of America* v. *Bennett, supra* note 31, at 1443.

[333.5] Los Angeles.

[333.6] *Gospel Missions of America* v. *Bennett, supra* note 31.

## § 5.11 · REGISTRATION FEES

pp. 422–423, last line. *Replace last sentence and carryover with:*

These fees must be tested against principles protecting free speech, in that freedom of expression must be "available to all, not merely to those who can pay their own way."[345.1] The courts have held that a "licensing fee to be used in defraying administrative costs is permissible, but only to the extent that the fees are necessary."[345.2] The constitutionality of this type of fee in the charitable solicitation setting was the subject of federal appellate court opinions issued in 1994 and 1995.

* p. 423, n. 347. *Replace "F.2d" with "F.3d".*

* p. 424, n. 358. *Insert following existing material:*

A similar sliding-scale fee structure in a county ordiance was upheld in *American Charities for Reasonable Fundraising Regulation, Inc.* v. *Pinellas County, supra* note 42.1.

p. 425, n. 367. *Insert following existing material:*

Subsequently, the requirements that a professional fund-raiser pay a $55 fee (and post a $5,000 bond) were found to directly restrain protected speech and thus were pronounced facially unconstitutional, because the government did not demonstrate a "link between the fee and the bond and the costs of the licensing process" (*Gospel Missions of America* v. *Bennett, supra* note 31, at 1447).

p. 425. *Following second complete paragraph, insert:*

* ## § 5.12 · CONCLUSIONS (NEW)

p. 425, last line. *Insert footnote at end of line:*

[369] State regulation of fund-raising (using that term in a broad sense) can occur in contexts not involving charitable solicitation acts. For example, at present, some state attorneys general are developing guidelines by which to regulate *marketing partnerships* between charitable organizations and for-profit businesses. A summary of this report is at XI *Chron. of Phil.* (No. 13) 48 (April 22, 1999). These arrangements entail charity endorsements or advertising that suggest that a charity is endorsing or warranting a product or service. A hearing was held in New York at the end of May on the proposal. In general, Giorgianni, "Charities Criticize Proposals to Regulate Marketing Deals," XI *Chron. of Phil.* (No. 16) 37 (June 3, 1999).

---

[345.1] *Murdock* v. *Pennsylvania, supra* note 286, at 111.

[345.2] *Fernandes* v. *Limmer, supra* note 242.1, at 633 (citations omitted). Also *Holy Spirit Association for Unification of World Christianity* v. *Hodge, supra* note 160, at 604.

# CHAPTER SIX

# Federal Regulation
# of Fund-Raising

## § 6.2 FUND-RAISING DISCLOSURE BY CHARITABLE ORGANIZATIONS

p. 436, n. 52. *Replace with:*
[52] See Appendix G.

p. 437, n. 53. *Replace with:*
[53] See Appendix H.

p. 437, n. 54. *Replace with:*
[54] See Appendix I.

## § 6.4 QUID PRO QUO CONTRIBUTION RULES

p. 442, n. 88. *Replace "6.3" with "6.2".*

## § 6.5 FUND-RAISING DISCLOSURE BY NONCHARITABLE ORGANIZATIONS

p. 446, n. 109. *Insert following existing material:*
See *Law of Tax-Exempt Organizations* Chapter 13.

p. 446, n. 110. *Insert following existing material:*
See *Law of Tax-Exempt Organizations* Chapter 15.

## § 6.6 THE UNRELATED BUSINESS RULES

p. 447, n. 112. *Replace "850-961" with "Chapters 26-28".*

### (a) Basic Concepts of Unrelated Income Taxation

p. 448, n. 120. *Replace "117-122" with "§ 4.5".*

p. 448, n. 125. *Replace "549-571" with "Chapter 12".*

p. 449, n. 126. *Replace "616-621" with "§ 15.1".*

p. 449, n. 127. *Replace "572-596" with "Chapter 13".*

p. 449, n. 128. *Replace "672-676" with "§ 18.4".*

p. 449, n. 129. *Replace "690-693" with "§ 18.10".*

p. 449, n. 130. *Replace "606-612, 857-858" with "§§ 14.3, 28.3".*

p. 449, n. 131. *Replace "597-615" with "Chapter 14".*

p. 449, n. 132. *Replace "702-704" with "§ 18.3".*

p. 449, n. 133. *Replace "648-664" with "Chapter 17".*

p. 449, n. 134. *Replace "665-666"with "§ 18.1".*

p. 449, n. 135. *Replace "229-232" with "§ 8.7".*

p. 449, n. 136. *Replace "693-701" with "§ 18.11".*

p. 449, n. 137. *Replace "701-702" with "§ 18.12".*

p. 449, n. 138. *Replace "666-670" with "§ 18.2".*

p. 449, n. 139. *Replace "477-485" with "§ 11.4(c)".*

p. 451, n. 148. *Replace "568-569" with "§ 22.1".*

p. 459, n. 199. *Insert following existing material:*

The IRS is of the view that this exception is not available where the solicitation is in competition with for-profit vendors or where the solicitation is illegal (Tech. Adv. Mem. 9652004).

p. 461, line 12. *Insert footnote following semicolon:*

[210.1] For the exclusion for rental income to apply, it is necessary that the underlying document be a *lease* rather than a *license* (IRS Priv. Ltr. Rul. 9740032).

p. 461, line 15. *Replace "may be" with "are".*

## (b) Unrelated Income Rules as Applied to Fund-Raising

p. 463, n. 227. *Replace "887-891" with "§ 26.5(a)(ii)".*

p. 464, n. 233. *Delete "accompanying" and substitute "accompanied by".*

p. 465, n. 241. *Insert following "Also":*

KJ's Fund Raisers, Inc. v. Commissioner, 74 T.C.M. 669 (1997);

p. 467, n. 253. *Replace "1179" with "1178".*

p. 473, n. 283. *Replace "249-263" with "§ 4.6".*

p. 473, n. 284. *Replace "264-299" with "Chapter 19".*

p. 475, n. 304. *Insert following existing material:*

In one of these instances, a tax-exempt organization sponsored a concert series open to the public occupying two weekends each year, one in the spring and one in the fall. The preparation and ticket solicitation for each of the concerts usually occupies up to six months. Taking into account the preparatory time involved, the IRS concluded that the concerts were unrelated business activities that were regularly carried on (Tech. Adv. Mem. 9712001).

p. 476. *Replace page with:*

the activity can be considered a tax-free royalty.[306] Because the term royalty is not defined in the Internal Revenue Code or the tax regulations, the scope of the term has been the subject of considerable litigation. There are essentially three ways to define the boundaries of what is a royalty, which basically is a payment for the right to use an item of intangible property: (1) as only a payment that is a form of investment income, when no services may be provided by the royalty recipient; (2) as only a payment that is a form of passive income, when an insubstantial amount of services may be provided by the royalty recipient; or (3) as any payment that constitutes a royalty irrespective of the extent of services the recipient of the royalty may provide.

The position of the IRS is that a royalty is excluded from unrelated business income taxation only when it satisfies the first of these definitions, that is, is investment income. Thus, the IRS asserts that if a charitable or other type of tax-exempt organization is actively participating in the undertaking that generates the income (such as promoting a product or service to its membership or making public endorsements), the organization is part of a joint venture and the exclusion for royalties is unavailable. This view has been

---

[306] See *supra* text accompanied by notes 202–209.

dramatically rejected by the U.S. Tax Court, which has held that, to be excludable from taxation, the income need only be a payment for the use of one or more valuable intangible property rights.[307] In one instance, that court held that revenue from the rental of mailing lists (where the statutory exception[308] was unavailable) was properly treated as a royalty.[309] In another, that court extended this analysis to income received from an affinity card program.[310]

The core of this interpretation of the royalty exception by the Tax Court is that, although Congress may have believed that royalties and similar types of excluded income are passive,[311] that does not necessarily mean that they must always, in fact, be passive.[312] Stated in the reverse, this view holds that a statutorily classified item of income excludable from tax remains excludable irrespective of whether the income is derived from an investment, is passive, or is generated from the active conduct of a trade or business.

As the consequence of an appeal of the Tax Court's findings, an opinion issued by the U.S. Court of Appeals for the Ninth Circuit in mid-1996 represents the most authoritative court analysis of this issue. Reviewing dictionary definitions of the term *royalty,* this appellate court concluded that a royalty is a payment for the right to use intangible property. However, in a sharp departure from the Tax Court approach, the court added that a royalty "cannot include compensation for services rendered by the owner of the property."[313] Thus, the Ninth Circuit adopted the second of the definitions as to the scope of the royalty exception.[314]

This definition is a compromise between the position taken by tax-exempt organizations and that of the IRS. The court of appeals wrote that, to

---

[307] *Disabled American Veterans* v. *Commissioner,* 94 T.C. 60 (1990), *rev'd on other grounds,* 942 F.2d 309 (6th Cir. 1991).

[308] See *supra* text accompanied by notes 200 and 233.

[309] *Sierra Club, Inc.* v. *Commissioner,* 65 T.C.M. 2582 (1993) ("*Sierra Club I*").

[310] *Sierra Club, Inc.* v. *Commissioner,* 103 T.C. 307 (1994) ("*Sierra Club II*"). Also *Oregon State University Alumni Ass'n, Inc.* v. *Commissioner,* 71 T.C.M. 1935 (1996); *Alumni Ass'n of the University of Oregon, Inc.* v. *Commissioner,* 71 T.C.M. 2093 (1996); *Mississippi State University Alumni, Inc.* v. *Commissioner,* 74 T.C.M. 458 (1997) (appeal not taken). For the position of the IRS with respect to affinity card programs, see *infra* text accompanied by notes 323–324.

[311] See *supra* quotation accompanied by note 207.

[312] This view is based on additional language in the committee reports indicating that the exception for dividends, interest, annuities, royalties, and the like "applies not only to investment income [as noted, the narrowest of the three definitions of excludable income], but also to such items as business interest on overdue open accounts receivable" (S. Rep. No. 2375, *supra* note 142, at 108; H.R. Rep. No. 2139, *supra* note 142, at 110).

[313] *Sierra Club, Inc.* v. *Commissioner,* 86 F.3d 1526, 1532 (9th Cir. 1996) ("*Sierra Club III*"). This element of the definition of a royalty is consistent with the long-time stance of the IRS that "royalties do not include payments for personal services" (Rev. Rul. 81-178, 1981-2 C.B. 135).

[314] There is precedent for this approach (*Disabled American Veterans* v. *United States, supra* note 253; *Fraternal Order of Police, Illinois State Troopers Lodge No. 41* v. *Commissioner,* 833 F.2d 717 (7th Cir. 1987); *Disabled American Veterans* v. *Commissioner, supra* note 307 (6th Cir.); *Texas Farm Bureau* v. *United States,* 53 F.3d 120 (5th Cir. 1995).

the extent the Service "claims that a tax-exempt organization can do *nothing* to acquire such fees," the agency is "incorrect."[314.1] Yet, "to the extent that . . . [an exempt organization] appears to argue that a 'royalty' is any payment for the use of a property right—such as a copyright—regardless of any additional services that are performed in addition to the owner simply permitting another to use the right at issue, we disagree."[314.2]

The Ninth Circuit's reading of the facts concerning the mailing list rentals favored the exempt organization in the litigation, which had contracted out many of the services involved in marketing and renting its lists. The court found that the organization "did nothing more than collect a fee" for these rentals.[314.3] The income received by the organization from the list rentals was held to be royalty income and not payment for services.[314.4] The circumstances concerning the affinity card program were afforded far different treatment. The appellate court disapproved of the way in which the Tax Court had resolved certain factual issues, namely, in favor of the exempt organization involved. This court also strongly suggested that the affinity card program fees were not excludable royalties, because of the extent of services provided.[314.5]

\*     The Tax Court decided the affinity card program case in mid-1999.[314.6] This case, therefore, turned on whether or not the exempt organization involved was rendering services in connection with the program. The organization, of course, had argued that its name, logo, and mailing list are intangible assets, and that pursuant to the agreement with the card services company it had licensed those properties to the company in exchange for payments that constitute royalties. The IRS asserted that the organization, in this connection, was in a business involving "marketing," "sponsoring," "promoting," and/or "endorsing" the credit card program. The government contended that the contracts entered into by the exempt organization were for services only and that the resulting income was not royalty income because the organization was being paid for these services.

\*     The Tax Court focused on the agreement between the organization and the card company. The provisions regulating the company's use of the exempt organization's name and marks were seen as being in the contract to preserve the organization's property interests in those items. The right to advise and consent with regard to the marketing material prepared by the company was viewed as a right intended to safeguard the organization's name, marks, logo, and other

---

[314.1] *Sierra Club III, supra* note 313, at 1535 (emphasis in original).

[314.2] *Id.*

[314.3] *Id.* at 1536.

\*  [314.4] Consequently, *Sierra Club I, supra* note 309, was affirmed by *Sierra Club III, supra* note 313.

[314.5] Consequently, *Sierra Club III, supra* note 310, was reversed by *Sierra Club III, supra* note 313, and the case remanded so that the Tax Court could once again make findings of fact and conclusions of law, this time following a trial rather than by grant of summary judgment. The trial was held in September 1997.

\*  [314.6] *Sierra Club, Inc.* v. *Commissioner,* 77 T.C.M. 1569 (1999) ("*Sierra Club IV*").

intangibles used in the marketing. Thus, the financial consideration the organization received under this agreement was held to be, at least in part, consideration for the use of valuable intangible property, and as such constituted royalties.

* The government asserted that the exempt organization provided seven types of services, all as part of the contention that it was in the business of marketing the credit card program to its members. None of these assertions was successful. One of these sets of asserted services was the organization's control over the marketing materials by way of its power to negate. Also, the organization was provided monthly accountings by the card company. Nonetheless, the court was moved by the fact that the organization did not receive a fee for any marketing activities and did not share in any economics realized by the company in its expenditures made in carrying out its marketing responsibilities.

* The Court expressly held that the exempt organization's rights in this regard were not inconsistent with a royalty arrangement. These rights were characterized as only evidencing the organization's concern with "protecting the worth of its property interest in its good name and marks."[314.7] It was held not to be an indirect method of putting the organization in the business of marketing.

* The court rejected the idea that the credit card was being offered by the organization as a member service. The bank involved was the financial institution that extended credit to the members, and it was the card company's marketing efforts that brought the possibility of the credit card and certain other services to the attention of the members. Mere endorsement of the program was held not to be a service provided by the organization.

* Although the card company advertised in the exempt organization's publications, it was not given any financial preferences. The company used the organization's nonprofit mail permit on one occasion but the court was convinced that that was a mistake. The license agreement, requiring the organization to "cooperate" with the company, was found by the court to "not [be] an agreement to endorse or promote the credit card program beyond the endorsement that necessarily results from [the organization's] license of its logo, name, and the other intangibles here in question."[314.8]

* In short, none of the receipts of this exempt organization were in consideration for services provided by the organization as part of the credit card program. All of the receipts were found to be in consideration for the use of the organization's valuable intangible property and, as such, constituted tax-excludable royalties.[314.9]

---

* [314.7] *Id.* at 1577.
* [314.8] *Id.* at 1578.
* [314.9] This decision can be appealed to the Ninth Circuit. It may be assumed that that appellate court would look carefully at the Tax Court's conclusion that the exempt organization was not being paid for any services rendered in conjunction with the affinity card program. Nonetheless, the Tax Court did a fine job of examining the innards of this credit card program; those entering into (or writing) contracts of this nature are well advised not to wander outside the parameters of the royalty exclusion articulated by the court, particularly until the next move of the IRS is known.

There is a vagary in the Ninth Circuit's opinion as to the range of the gap between merely collecting a fee (with no activities) and the amount of tolerable activity the court seemingly contemplates within the boundaries as to what constitutes an excludable royalty. In the context of mailing list rentals, two examples were offered: provision of a rate sheet listing the fee charged for use of each copyrighted design, and retention of the right to approve how the design is used and marketed. Activities that are problematic in this area in general are endorsements, use of the tax-exempt organization's postal permit to send solicitation materials, publishing of paid advertising, the right of the exempt organization to advise with respect to marketing materials, sorting mailing lists, provision of list information on magnetic tape or labels, and provision of other clerical, telephone, and administrative services.[314.10]

During the pendency of this litigation, the IRS is holding to its views in its rulings. For example, the IRS ruled that payments by a commercial enterprise for use of the name and logo of a charitable organization are taxable as unrelated business income (and are not excludable royalties) because the charity also provided endorsements of the business's services.[314.11]

Charitable organizations must, until this point of law is further clarified, decide whether to follow the view of the IRS, the Ninth Circuit, or the Tax Court as to the scope of the royalty exclusion, and structure (or restructure) their endeavors to utilize the royalty exception. One current practice—as yet not commented upon by the IRS and untested in the courts—is to create two (or three) contracts: one pertaining to the performance of services (the income from which would likely be taxable) and one for the mere use of intangible property (to establish a basis for the assertion that this element of the income is a nontaxable royalty).

* p. 477. *Insert as second paragraph:*

One of the arguments persistently advanced by the IRS is that statutory exception protecting certain mailing list transactions from taxation is to be

---

* [314.10] In the aftermath of the Ninth Circuit's decision, the Tax Court ruled that payments received by a tax-exempt organization for the use of its mailing list are not subject to unrelated business income taxation because they constitute royalties (*Common Cause* v. *Commissioner*, 112 T.C. No. 23 (1999)). The rental lists are stored at a computer service business and the exempt organization retains the services of a list manager and list broker. Payments from mailers are remitted by the list manager to the organization, less the manager's and broker's commissions and payments to the computer house. With one exception, all of the activities of the parties were deemed to be *royalty-related*, that is, designed to exploit or protect the exempt organization's intangible property. Certain activities provided solely to mailers by list brokers were found not to be royalty-related. The court also concluded that none of these parties were functioning as agents of the exempt organization, so none of the activities and payments were attributable to the exempt organization. See also *Planned Parenthood Federation of America, Inc.* v. *Commissioner*, 77 T.C.M. 2227 (1999).

[314.11] IRS Priv. Ltr. Rul. 9450028. In subsequent rulings, the IRS has found a royalty to be present (Priv. Ltr. Ruls. 9816027, 9709029, and 9703025) and not present (Tech. Adv. Mem. 9723001; Priv. Ltr. Rul. 9810030).

read as permitting (perhaps requiring) taxation of these transactions in situations where the exception is not available. This contention is equally persistently rejected in the courts.[321.1] The legislative history of the provision is to the contrary of the IRS position. One element of this history states as follows: "No inference is intended as to whether or not revenues from mailing list activities other than those described in the provision, or from mailing list activities described in the provision, but occurring prior to the effective date, constitute unrelated business income."[321.2] This point was also reflected in the House debate on the legislation, in remarks offered by the then-Chairman of the House Committee on Ways and Means: this provision "carries no inference whatever that mailing list revenues beyond its scope or prior to its effective date should be considered taxable to an exempt organization."[321.3]

p. 478, line 1. *Insert "credit" before "card".*

p. 478, line 1. *Insert footnote following comma:*

[322.1] One court defined an affinity credit card program as "an arrangement by which an organization such as Sierra Club agrees that a credit card issuer may use the organization's name and logo to market an affinity credit card—i.e., the Sierra Club Visa Card—in exchange for a small percentage of total amounts charged on the affinity card" (*Sierra Club, III, supra* note 313, at 1528 n. 2).

p. 478, n. 324, line 1. *Replace "314" with "314.7".*

## § 6.7 EXEMPTION APPLICATION PROCESS

### (b) The Application Procedure

p. 479. *Delete first paragraph and substitute:*

The IRS has promulgated specific rules by which a ruling or determination letter may be issued to an organization in response to the filing of an application for recognition of its tax-exempt status. An organization seeking recognition of exemption should file the application with the IRS Service Center in Cincinnati, Ohio. Usually, the determination of exemption will be made at that level. However, if the application presents a matter of some controversy or an unresolved or novel point of law, the application will be

---

\* [321.1] E.g., *Common Cause v. Commissioner, supra* note 314.10.
\* [321.2] Staff of Joint Comm. on Taxation, *General Explanation of the Tax Reform Act of 1986* 1325 (J. Comm. Print 1987).
\* [321.3] 132 *Cong. Rec.* 26208 (Sept. 25, 1986).

sent on to the headquarters of the IRS in Washington, D.C., for resolution at that level.

p. 479, n. 330. *Replace with*:

330 Rev. Proc. 90-27, 1990-1 C.B. 514. See *Law of Tax-Exempt Organizations* § 23.2.

### (c)  The Application

p. 481, n. 333. *Replace "717-719, 1034-1035" with "§ 4.1".*

p. 482, n. 334. *Replace "733-737" with "§ 23.3".*

p. 482, n. 335. *Replace "1980-1 C.B. 119" with "supra note 328".*

p. 482, n. 336. *Replace "509-515" with "§ 11.4(e)".*

p. 484, n. 341. *Replace "520-528" with "§ 11.4(f)".*

### § 6.8  REPORTING REQUIREMENTS

p. 485, first paragraph. *Insert as last sentence*:

These returns are filed with the IRS Service Center in Ogden, Utah.

p. 485, n. 345. *Replace "763-781" with "§ 24.3".*

### *  (h)  Public Inspection

p. 490. *Insert at end of subsection:*

These public inspection rules have largely been superseded by document disclosure requirements that took effect in 1999.[360.1]

---

* 360.1 See *infra* § 6.22.

## (i)   Penalties

p. 490, line 2. *Replace "$10" with "$20".*

p. 490, line 3. *Replace "$5,000" with "$10,000".*

p. 490, first paragraph. *Insert as last sentence*:

In the case of an organization with gross receipts exceeding $1 million for a year, as to an annual information return for that year, the penalty is $100 a day, with the maximum penalty set at $50,000.

p. 490, n. 362. *Replace "652" with "6652".*

## § 6.9   LOBBYING RESTRICTIONS

p. 491, n. 365. *Replace "300-314" with "§ 20.3".*

p. 491, n. 367. *Replace material following first period with "See Law of Tax-Exempt Organizations § 20.5".*

## § 6.10   THE PUBLIC CHARITY CLASSIFICATIONS

p. 495, n. 385. *Replace "737-742" with "§ 23.4".*

p. 496, n. 393. *Replace "374-376" with "§ 11.3(b)(i)-(iii)".*

p. 497, n. 395. *Replace "377-386" with "§ 11.3(b)(iv)".*

p. 497, n. 397. *Replace "368" with "§ 11.3(b)(v)".*

p. 497, n. 398. *Replace "Chapters 20-25" with "§ 11.4".*

## § 6.12   FUND-RAISING COMPENSATION ARRANGEMENTS

p. 499, n. 411. *Replace "264-299" with "Chapter 19".*

## § 6.13  CHARITABLE DEDUCTION RULES

### (a)  Meaning of Gift

p. 504, n. 442. *Replace text with*:

442 According to the tax regulations, no part of a payment that an individual makes to or for the use of a charitable organization, that is in consideration for goods or services, is a gift for income tax deductibility purposes unless the individual intended to make a payment in an amount that exceeds the fair market value of the goods or services received (in which case only that excess amount can be a deductible gift) and the individual actually made that type of a payment (Reg. § 1.170A-1(h)(1), (2)). This places greater emphasis on donative intent than was previously the case.

p. 504. *Insert at end of subsection:*

Normally, contributions of money are made with after-tax dollars, that is, with funds that were first taxable as income; it is a rare opportunity when a charitable deduction can be accomplished with before-tax funds. In one such instance, the IRS ruled that a holder of a certain credit card makes a deductible charitable gift when a percentage of the price of an item (less an administration fee) purchased with the card at a participating retailer is transferred to a charitable organization selected by the cardholder.442.1

A company is to sponsor a line of credit and debit cards, to be identified by the company's name. These cards will be issued to cardholders throughout the United States by banks entering into license agreements with the company. The banks may charge an annual fee to their cardholders. The company will negotiate agreements with retailers, pursuant to which a percentage of the purchase price will be transferred to the company when one of these cards is used to purchase an item from a participating retailer. When they first receive their company cards and periodically thereafter, cardholders will receive a list of participating retailers. They will also be informed of the percentage of the retail purchase price that each participating retailer will pay to the company.

After a sale by a participating retailer to a cardholder, the agreed-upon percentage of the purchase price will be transferred by the bank (or its agent) processing the transaction to the company. Of this amount, an administration fee—approximately 20 percent—will be retained by the company. The balance of the amount transferred to the company will be transferred to a custodial account maintained by the company on behalf of each cardholder; these amounts are known as *rebates*.

When they apply for a card, applicants are asked to designate a charitable organization (one named in the IRS's cumulative list of charities442.2) to which they want to have their rebates paid. Cardholders are free to change

442.1 IRS Priv. Ltr. Rul. 9623035.
442.2 IRS Publication 78.

their designations at any time by notifying the company in writing. Rebates earned will appear as a line item on the cardholders' monthly statements from the issuing banks. If the cardholder returns to the retailer an item of merchandise purchased with one of these cards, the amount of the corresponding rebate will be deducted from the rebate amount held in the cardholders' custodial account. At the end of each calendar quarter, the company will transfer rebates that have accumulated in the custodial account to the charitable organization selected by the cardholder. For the fourth calendar quarter, these transfers will be made before the end of the calendar year.

The cardholders will not receive anything in exchange for the payments to charitable organizations of their rebates. However, instead of having the company pay their rebates to a charitable organization, cardholders may obtain the rebates for their personal use. Unless they advise the company in writing of their intention to obtain the rebates for themselves, cardholders' rebates will automatically be paid over to the designated charities.

When the company makes a payment to a charitable organization on behalf of a cardholder, the company will provide the organization with the amount of the cardholder's contribution, together with the cardholder's name and address. The company will also provide each cardholder with an annual statement reflecting the total amount transferred to a charitable organization with respect to that cardholder, along with the amount of each quarterly transfer.

The first issue resolved by the IRS was whether the rebates paid to a charitable organization are deductible by the cardholder as a charitable contribution. The answer: yes. The IRS pointed out that a charitable gift must be made voluntarily and with charitable intent. In this situation, those requirements are met, in that cardholders have the choice of directing the company to refund rebates to them or transfer the rebates to a charitable organization. Moreover, the cardholders also have the opportunity to select the charitable organizations that will receive their rebates.

The IRS ruled that the opportunity to decide whether payments will be made to a charity, together with the ability to designate the charity to receive the payments, renders the payments voluntary. Hence, the directed rebates are deductible charitable gifts.

In almost every charitable gift situation involving money, the contribution is made with after-tax dollars. That is, the funds must first be taken into income before they can be deductible when transferred to charity. Here, however, the IRS concluded that a rebate paid by a retailer participating in the card program is not income to the cardholder. Rather, the rebate reflects a reduction in the purchase price paid for an item purchased with the company's card.

The IRS's holding in this regard is based on a 1976 revenue ruling.[442.3] That ruling stated that rebates paid by an automobile manufacturer to qualify-

---

[442.3] Rev. Rul. 76-96, 1976-1 C.B. 23.

ing retail customers who purchase new automobiles are not includible in the gross income of the customers.

The third issue addressed by the IRS was the timing of the charitable deduction. The Service ruled that a cardholder may claim the deduction for the tax year in which the company made payments to one or more charitable organizations on the cardholder's behalf. Under these facts, the company is not functioning as an agent for the donee charities. Instead, the company serves as the agent for the cardholders with respect to the rebate amounts it holds. Thus, although the rebates are held by the company, the cardholders retain control over them.

For a charitable gift to be deductible, there must be the requisite delivery. It is not enough for there to be delivery to a party for subsequent delivery to a charitable organization. Accordingly, there is no delivery of a charitable contribution when the company receives the rebate amounts, nor when the cardholders fail to claim rebates for their personal use. Rather, delivery occurs when the company transfers the rebate funds to the designated charities. (If the company served as the agent of the charities, the deduction would arise at the time the company received the rebate amounts.) This program is designed to allow individuals to have the charitable deduction in the year of the rebate by enabling the company to transfer the rebates to charity before the close of the tax year.

The final issue was application of the substantiation rules.[442.4] The IRS ruled that, in the case of a lump-sum payment of $250 or more by the company to a charitable organization, the cardholder must obtain the requisite substantiation of the gift from the charity for the gift to be deductible. This is an application of the rule that separate payments are generally treated as separate contributions and will not be aggregated for purposes of applying the $250 threshold.

The company indicated to the IRS that it intends to supply donee charitable organizations with the amounts of cardholders' contributions, as well as the names and addresses of the cardholders. The IRS said that, with this information, the charities can provide the contemporaneous written acknowledgment required by the substantiation rules.[442.5]

---

[442.4] See *supra* § 6.3.

[442.5] This card program may seem strikingly similar to the group insurance premium refund program that the Supreme Court ruled, in 1986, did not give rise to deductible gifts (*United States* v. *American Bar Endowment*) (see *supra* § 6.6). In that case, a membership organization maintained a group insurance program for its members. Every year, a portion of the insurance premiums paid was refunded to the organization. As a condition of participating in the insurance program, members were required to assign refunds from their premiums to the organization, which in turn used the refunds for charitable ends. The Supreme Court held that members participating in the group insurance program could not have a charitable contribution deduction for their pro rata shares of the refund amounts that funded charitable activities. The deductions were disallowed because the payments were not voluntary.

## (e)    Deduction Reduction Rules

p. 508, third paragraph, last sentence. *Replace (other than footnote) with:*

However, individuals were allowed to base their charitable contribution deductions for gifts of certain publicly traded securities to private foundations on the full fair market value of the property, although this special rule does not apply with respect to qualified securities contributed after December 31, 1994, and before July 1, 1996, or after June 30, 1998. This rule as to qualified appreciated securities was made permanent in 1998.

p. 508, n. 467, line 1. *Replace "charitable organization in 1994" with "private foundation in a year in which this rule is in effect."*

p. 508, n. 467, line 3. *Insert "in an appropriate subsequent year, including one in which the rule is not in effect" before parenthesis.*

p. 508, n. 467, line 4. *Delete "and"; insert ", 9734034, and 9812030" before parenthesis at end of note.*

## (f)    "Twice Basis" Deductions

p. 509, third paragraph. *Insert as second sentence:*

Also, a similar rule applies with respect to gifts of computer technology and equipment for elementary or secondary school purposes, in the case of contributions made after December 31, 1997, and before January 1, 2000.[469.1]

## (h)    Partial Interest Gifts

p. 511, n. 487. *Replace "1994-32 I.R.B. 15" with "1994-2 C.B. 555".*

---

The key difference in this case was that the rebate transfers are voluntary: the cardholders have a clear choice to receive the refunds or donate them to charity. In the group insurance program, by contrast, those who wished to participate in it could not decline to have their premium refunds transferred to a charitable organization.

Also, as to the insurance program, the recipient charitable organization was selected by the sponsoring organization. In this case, the cardholders select the charitable beneficiaries of the rebates.

[469.1] IRC § 170(e)(6).

p. 511, n. 489. *Replace "1995-2 I.R.B. 15" with "1995-1 C.B. 288".*

## § 6.15 APPLICATION OF THE COMMENSURATE TEST

p. 523, line 4. *Insert "unsuccessfully" following "subsequently".*

p. 523, n. 565. *Replace citation with:*
", 109 T.C. 326 (1997)".

### (b) Law and Analysis

\* p. 526, n. 569. *Replace text following comma with:*
supra note 415.

p. 526, n. 570. *Replace "Chapter 13, particularly § 13.7" with "§§ 19.3, 19.10".*

### (d) Status of the Litigation

p. 528, first paragraph. *Replace last sentence with:*
The opinion in this case was issued on December 2, 1997.

p. 528, n. 580. *Replace "788-790" with "§ 24.6(a)".*

p. 528, n. 581. *Replace "790-802" with "§ 24.6(b)".*

p. 529. *Insert at end of section:*

### (e) Summary of the Opinion (New)

The opinion of the Tax Court in this case did not address the commensurate test. However, the court agreed with the IRS that private inurement occurred, in that the fund-raising firm was paid excessive compensation and manipulated assets of the charitable organization (principally its mailing list) for its private ends. The firm was found to be an insider with respect to the charitable organization since it exercised "substantial control" over the charity's finances and direct-mail fund-raising campaigns over several years.[584.1]

The court observed that the charity was "heavily financed and kept in existence" by the fund-raising company by reason of the fund-raising arrangement they had.[584.2] This relationship, wrote the court, "was in many ways analogous to that of a founder and major contributor to a new organization."[584.3]

The contract between the parties was bargained for, the court conceded, but that factor alone did not, wrote the court, "by itself conclusively protect an arrangement from a determination that the compensation was unreasonable."[584.4] Sensitive to the implications of this finding, the court added: "We are not holding that an arm's-length arrangement that produces a poor result for an organization necessarily would cause the organization to lose its tax-exempt status."[584.5]

\* This decision by the Tax Court was, however, reversed on appeal. The U.S. Court of Appeals for the Seventh Circuit concluded that the fund-raising firm was not an insider with respect to the public charity.[584.6] The appellate court said it could not find anything in the facts to support the "theory" that the fund-raising company "seized control of UCC and by doing so became an insider."[584.7] The case was remanded to the Tax Court for consideration in view of the doctrine of private benefit.[584.8]

## § 6.17 SPECIAL EVENTS AND CORPORATE SPONSORSHIPS

### (c) Proposed Legislation

p. 546. *Delete last paragraph of section, including footnote.*

---

[584.1] *United Cancer Council, Inc.* v. *Commissioner, supra* note 565, at 388. Elsewhere in the opinion, the court observed that the fund-raising company had "extensive control" over the charity (*id.*).

[584.2] *Id.* at 387.

[584.3] *Id.*

[584.4] *Id.* at 396.

[584.5] *Id.* (The Tax Court subsequently held that a charitable organization's tax exemption should not be forfeited on grounds of private inurement where an insider embezzled funds from it (*Variety Club Tent No. 6 Charities, Inc.* v. *Commissioner,* 74 T.C.M. 1485 (1997)). The *United Cancer Council* case is also the subject of §§ 8.12 and 8.15C.

\* [584.6] *United Cancer Council, Inc.* v. *Commissioner,* 165 F.3d 1173 (7th Cir. 1999).

\* [584.7] *Id.* at 1178.

\* [584.8] The Tax Court has held that a transaction that amounts to private inurement also constitutes private benefit (*American Campaign Academy* v. *Commissioner, supra* note 569). (The private benefit doctrine is the subject of *supra* § 6.15(b)(iii).) Impermissible private benefit arises when it is more than insubstantial; it is unlikely that the Tax Court will find the private benefits in this case to be insubstantial.

## (d)  Proposed Regulation

p. 549. *Delete last paragraph of section, including footnote.*

p. 549. *Insert at end of section*:

## (e)  Enacted Legislation (New)

Enactment of legislation in 1997 added to the federal tax statutory law the concept of the qualified sponsorship payment.[697.1] These payments received by tax-exempt organizations and state colleges and universities are exempt from the unrelated business income tax. That is, the activity of soliciting and receiving these payments is not an unrelated business.[697.2]

From the standpoint of fund-raising, these rules differentiate between a *qualified sponsorship payment*, which is a deductible charitable contribution and as to which there is merely an acknowledgment, and a payment for services that are, or are in the nature of, advertising.

A qualified sponsorship payment is a payment made by a person engaged in a trade or business, with respect to which there is no arrangement or expectation that the person will receive any substantial return benefit other than the use or acknowledgment of the name or logo (or product lines) of the person's trade or business in connection with the organization's activities.[697.3] It is irrelevant whether the sponsored activity is related or unrelated to the organization's exempt purpose.[697.4]

This use or acknowledgment does not include advertising of the person's products or services, including messages containing qualitative or comparative language, price information or other indications of savings or value, an endorsement, or an inducement to purchase, sell, or use the products or services.[697.5] For example, if in return for receiving a sponsorship payment, an exempt organization promises to use the sponsor's name or logo in acknowledging the sponsor's support for an educational or fund-raising event conducted by the organization, the payment is not taxable. However, if an organization provides advertising of a sponsor's products, the payment made to the organization by the sponsor to receive the advertising is subject to the

---

[697.1] Taxpayer Relief Act of 1997, § 965(a).

[697.2] IRC § 513(i)(1).

[697.3] IRC § 513(i)(2)(A).

[697.4] H. Rep. No. 105-220, 105th Cong., 1st Sess. 69 (1997).

[697.5] IRC § 513(i)(2)(A).

unrelated business income tax (assuming the other requirements for taxation are satisfied).[697.6]

A qualified sponsorship payment does not include any payment where the amount of the payment is contingent on the level of attendance at one or more events, broadcast ratings, or other factors indicating the degree of public exposure to one or more events.[697.7] However, the fact that a sponsorship payment is contingent on an event actually taking place or being broadcast, in and of itself, does not cause the payment to fail to qualify. Also, mere distribution or display of a sponsor's products by the sponsor or the exempt organization to the general public at a sponsored event, whether for free or for remuneration, is considered a "use or acknowledgment" of the sponsor's product lines—and not advertising.[697.8]

This law does not apply to a payment which entitles the payor to the use or acknowledgment of the name or logo (or product line) of the payor's trade or business in a tax-exempt organization's periodical. A *periodical* is regularly scheduled and printed material published by or on behalf of the payee organization that is not related to and primarily distributed in connection with a specific event conducted by the payee organization.[697.9] Thus, the exclusion does not apply to payments that lead to acknowledgments in a monthly journal but applies if a sponsor received an acknowledgment in a program or brochure distributed at a sponsored event.[697.10] The term *qualified sponsorship payment* also does not include a payment made in connection with a qualified convention or trade show activity.[697.11]

To the extent a portion of a payment would (if made as a separate payment) be a qualified sponsorship payment, that portion of the payment is treated as a separate payment; that is, a payment may be bifurcated as between an excludable amount and a nonexcludable amount.[697.12] Therefore, if a sponsorship payment made to a tax-exempt organization entitles the sponsor to product advertising and use or acknowledgment of the sponsor's name or logo by the organization, the unrelated business income tax does not apply to the amount of the payment that exceeds the fair market value of the product advertising provided to the sponsor.[697.13]

The provision of facilities, services, or other privileges by an exempt organization to a sponsor or the sponsor's designees (such as complimentary tickets, Pro-Am playing spots in golf tournaments, or receptions for major

---

[697.6] H. Rep. No. 105-220, *supra* note 697.3, at 68.

[697.7] IRC § 513(i)(2)(B)(i).

[697.8] H. Rep. No. 105-220, *supra* note 697.3, at 69.

[697.9] IRC § 513(i)(2)(B)(ii)(I).

[697.10] H. Rep. No. 105-220, *supra* note 697.3, at 69.

[697.11] IRC § 513(i)(2)(B)(ii)(II).

[697.12] IRC § 513(i)(3).

[697.13] H. Rep. No. 105-220, *supra* note 697.3, at 69.

donors) in connection with a sponsorship payment does not affect the determination as to whether the payment is a qualified one. Instead, the provision of the goods or services is evaluated as a separate transaction in determining whether the organization has unrelated business income from the event. In general, if the services or facilities do not constitute a substantial return benefit (or if the provision of the services or facilities is a related business activity), the payments attributable to them are not subject to the unrelated business income tax.[697.14]

Likewise, a sponsor's receipt of a license to use an intangible asset (such as a trademark, logo, or designation) of the tax-exempt organization is treated as separate from the qualified sponsorship transaction in determining whether the organization has unrelated business taxable income.[697.15]

This statutory exemption from taxation for qualified sponsorship payments is in addition to other exemptions from the unrelated business income tax. These exceptions include the one for activities substantially all the work for which is performed by volunteers[697.16] and for activities not regularly carried on.[697.17]

Proposed regulations to accompany this legislation are expected in 1998. These regulations are expected to bear considerable resemblance to those proposed in 1993,[697.18] inasmuch as the statute is based in considerable part on the proposal.

p. 549. *Transfer text of footnote 697 to follow material in footnote 696.*

## § 6.18 IRS AS CONSUMER ADVISOR

p. 550, n. 701. *Replace "1995-6 I.R.B. 36" with "1995-1 C.B. 292".*

p. 550, n. 701. *Replace "1995-16 I.R.B. 12" with "1995-1 C.B. 300".*

p. 550, n. 702. *Replace "1995-23 I.R.B. 10" with "1995-1 C.B. 309".*

[697.14] *Id.*
[697.15] *Id.*
[697.16] See *supra* § 6.6(vi).
[697.17] See *supra* § 6.6(iv). This law became effective with respect to qualified sponsorship payments solicited or received after December 31, 1997. There is no inference as to whether a sponsorship payment received prior to 1998 was taxable.
[697.18] See *supra* § 6.17(d).

## § 6.20 THE POSTAL LAWS

p. 550, n. 703. *Replace "1995-35 I.R.B. 17" with "1995-2 C.B. 331".*

## § 6.20 THE POSTAL LAWS

* p. 552, second line of section. *Insert "to a significant extent" following "regulated".*

* p. 552, second line. *Replace "is done" with "regulation is largely accomplished".*

* p. 552, third line. *Delete " , reduced bulk third-class".*

* p. 552, lines 6–7. *Replace "third-class" with "special".*

## * (a) Introduction

p. 553, fifth line. *Delete "third-class".*

p. 553, first full paragraph, first line. *Insert "for nonprofit organizations" following "rate".*

p. 553, n. 731. *Replace "727" with "728".*

p. 553, first full paragraph, last line. *Replace "paid" with "absorbed".*

p. 553, second full paragraph, third line. *Insert "the government's" following the second "for".*

p. 553, second full paragraph, fourth line. *Replace "necessary funds" with "funds necessary to support the revenue forgone subsidy".*

p. 553, second full paragraph, last sentence. *Replace with:*

Absent "full funding" of revenue forgone, the USPS was authorized to raise the nonprofit postal rates.

p. 553, third full paragraph, fourth line. *Insert "in the nonprofit rates" following "increases".*

p. 553, third full paragraph, seventh line. *Insert "as to the revenue forgone amounts" following "community".*

p. 553, third full paragraph, eighth line. *Insert "the burden of" following "bear".*

p. 553, third full paragraph, last line. *Insert "in the applicable postal rates" following "increase".*

p. 553. *Insert as fifth complete paragraph, before heading:*

Today, the special rate for nonprofit organizations is termed by the USPS the *nonprofit standard mail rate.*

### (b) Qualifying Organizations

\* p. 553, first paragraph, first line. *Replace "special third-class" with "nonprofit standard mail".*

\* p. 554, n. 734, second line. *Replace "48 (Jan. 1, 1995" with "54 (July 1, 1999".*

\* p. 554, n. 734, third line. *Replace "370" with "670".*

p. 554, n. 735. *Replace "195-198" with "§ 7.2".*

\* p. 555, first full paragraph, sixth line. *Insert "the foregoing purposes or for" following "of".*

\* p. 555, first full paragraph, ninth line. *Replace "a philanthropy" with "an organization".*

\* p. 555, first full paragraph, eleventh line. *Replace "special bulk" with "nonprofit standard mail".*

\* p. 556, first line. *Replace "special bulk" with "nonprofit standard mail".*

\* p. 556, n. 736. *Replace "370" with "670".*

\* p. 556, n. 737. *Replace "4.0" with "4.1".*

\* p. 556, line 9. *Replace "special bulk" with "nonprofit standard mail".*

\* p. 556, n. 738. *Insert ", part 4.2." following existing material.*


\* **(c)   Application for Authorization**

p. 556, first paragraph, lines 1 and 2. *Replace "special bulk third-class" with "nonprofit standard mail".*

p. 556, n. 739, last line. *Replace "370.8.1" with "670.8.0".*

p. 556, *Delete footnote 741.*

p. 556, fifth paragraph, last sentence. *Replace "special bulk" with "nonprofit standard mail".*

p. 557, second paragraph, line 1. *Replace "special bulk" with "nonprofit standard mail".*

p. 557, second paragraph, line 3. *Replace "regular third-class" with "certain other".*

p. 557, second paragraph, line 4. *Delete "bulk third-class".*

p. 557, second paragraph, line 5. *Replace "special bulk third-class" with "nonprofit standard mail".*

p. 557, second paragraph, last sentence. *Replace "single-piece third class" with "the certain other".*

p. 557, third paragraph, line 1. *Replace "special bulk" with "nonprofit standard mail".*

p. 557, n. 743. *Replace "370" with "670".*

p. 557, n. 744. *Replace "370" with "670".*

## * (d) Eligible and Ineligible Matter

p. 558, first paragrpah, line 1. *Replace "special bulk" with "nonprofit standard mail".*

p. 558, second paragraph, line 1. *Replace "special bulk" with "nonprofit standard mail".*

p. 558, third paragraph, line 1. *Replace "special bulk third-class" with "nonprofit standard mail".*

p. 558, third paragraph, line 2. *Insert "or other" before "consideration".*

p. 558, numbered list, line 3. *Replace "special third-class" with "nonprofit standard mail".*

p. 558, n. 747. *Replace "3636" with "3626".*

p. 559, n. 748. *Replace "370" with "670".*

p. 559, n. 749. *Replace "370.5.6" with "670.5.7".*

p. 559, third full paragraph, lines 1 and 2. *Replace "special bulk third-class" with "nonprofit standard mail".*

p. 559, third full paragraph, line 5. *Insert "or other" before "consideration".*

p. 559, third full paragraph, line 7. *Replace "special bulk third-class" with "nonprofit standard mail".*

p. 560, n. 751. *Replace "(i)" with "(I)"; replace "3705.5.4d" with "670.5.6a".*

p. 560, second line. *Insert new paragraph before first full sentence:*

To be *substantially related*, the sale of the product or the provision of the service must contribute importantly to the accomplishment of one or more of the qualifying purposes of the organization. This means that the sale of the product or the provision of the service must be directly related to the accomplishment of one or more of the purposes on which the organization's authorization to mail at the nonprofit standard rates is based. The sale of the product or the provision of the service must have a causal relationship to the achievement of the exempt purposes (other than through the production of income) of the authorized organization. The selling of a product or service is not a related activity simply because the resulting income is used to accomplish the purpose of the aurhorized organization.

p. 560, n. 752. *Replace "370" with "670".*

p. 560, n. 753. *Replace "370.5.6(b)(2)" with "670.5.6b".*

p. 560, n. 756. *Replace "370.5.10" with "670.5.11".*

p. 560. *Insert after first full paragraph:*

To be a *periodical publication,* the material mailed must have a title (printed on the front cover page in a style and size of type that make it distinguishable from other information on the front cover page), be formed of printed sheets, contain an identification statement on one of the first five pages of the publication, and consist of at least 25 percent nonadvertising matter in each issue.[757.1]

Announcements for premiums received as a result of a contribution or payment of membership dues are not considered advertisements if the membership dues or requested contribution is more than four times the cost of the premium item(s) offered and more than two times the represented value in the mailpiece, if any, of the premium item(s) offered.

p. 560, second full paragraph, line 1. *Replace "special bulk" with "nonprofit standard mail".*

p. 560, n. 757. *Delete sentence following citation.*

p. 560, n. 758. *Replace "370.5.8" with "670.5.13, 11.1".*

p. 560, third full paragraph, first line. *Replace "special bulk" with "nonprofit standard mail".*

\* **(e)   Mailing Statement**

p. 560, first paragraph, first line. *Replace "special-rate bulk third-class" with "nonprofit standard rate".*

---

\*   [757.1] DMM E670.5.8.

p. 562. *Insert new section:*

## * § 6.22 DOCUMENT DISCLOSURE REQUIREMENTS (NEW)

The annual returns filed by charitable (and other tax-exempt) organizations[764] and the application for recognition of tax exemption[765] are now accessible to the public. This means that considerable information about the programs, income, expenses—and fund-raising activities—of charitable organizations is now easily and openly available to donors, other supporters, representatives of the media, and others. It may be anticipated that this deluge of information will have an impact on charitable fund-raising.

The IRS, in mid-1999, issued final regulations that provide guidelines for the disclosure of annual information returns and applications for recognition of tax exemption by exempt organizations, and that detail ways to utilize exceptions from these rules.[766] The effective date of these regulations is June 8, 1999.

Under this new regime, the general rules are that a tax-exempt organization must do the following:

- It must make its application for recognition of tax exemption available for public inspection without charge at its principal, regional, and district offices during regular business hours.
- It must make its annual information returns available for public inspection without charge in the same offices during regular business hours. Each return must be made available for a period of three years, beginning on the date the return is required to be filed or is actually filed, whichever is later.
- It must provide a copy without charge, other than a reasonable fee for reproduction and actual postage costs, of all or any part of any application or return required to be made available for public inspection to any individual who makes a request for the copy in person or in writing.

These rules[767] do not, at this time, apply to private foundations. Separate regulations are being prepared for foundations and eventually they will be encompassed by these disclosure requirements.

An *application for recognition of exemption* includes Form 1023 and 1024, and supporting documents. The term does not include an application

---

[764] See *supra* § 6.8.
[765] See *supra* § 6.7.
[766] T.D. 8818.
[767] Reg. § 301.6104(d)-3(a).

filed before July 15, 1987, unless the organization that filed it had a copy of it on that date. The *annual information return* generally means Forms 990 or 990-EZ.[768]

Generally, a tax-exempt organization must provide copies of the documents, in response to an in-person request, at its principal, regional, and district offices during regular business hours. Also generally, the organization must provide the copies to a requestor on the day the request is made.

In the case of an in-person request, when unusual circumstances mean that fulfillment of the request on the same business day would place an unreasonable burden of the exempt organization, the copies must be provided on the next business day following the day on which the unusual circumstances cease to exist or the fifth business day after the date of the request, whichever occurs first. *Unusual circumstances* include receipt of a volume of requests that exceeds the organization's daily capacity to make copies, requests received shortly before the end of regular business hours that require an extensive amount of copying, and requests received on a day when the organization's managerial staff capable of fulfilling the request is conducting special duties. *Special duties* are activities such as student registration or attendance at an off-site meeting or convention, rather than regular administrative duties.

If a request for a document is made in writing, the tax-exempt organization must honor it if the request:

- Is addressed to, and delivered by mail, electronic mail, facsimile, or a private delivery service to a principal, regional, or district office of the organization.
- Sets forth the address to which the copy of the document should be sent.

A tax-exempt organization receiving a written request for a copy must mail it within 30 days from the date the organization receives the request. If, however, an exempt organization requires payment in advance, it is only required to provide the copy within 30 days from the date it receives payment. A tax-exempt organization must fulfill a request for a copy of the organization's entire application or annual information return or any specific part or schedule of its application or return.

A tax-exempt organization may charge a reasonable fee for providing copies. A fee is *reasonable* if it is no more than the per-page copying fee charged by the IRS for providing copies. It can also include actual postage costs. The requestor may be required to pay the fee in advance.[769]

---

[768] Reg. § 301.6104(d)-3(b).
[769] Reg. § 301.6104(d)-3(d).

If a tax-exempt organization denies an individual's request for inspection or a copy of an application or return, and the individual wishes to alert the IRS to the possible need for enforcement action, he or she may send a statement to the appropriate IRS district office, describing the reason why the individual believes the denial was in violation of these requirements.[770] There are penalties for failure to comply with these rules.[771]

A tax-exempt organization is not required to comply with requests for copies of its application for recognition of tax exemption or an annual information return if the organization has made the document widely available.[772] The rules as to public inspection of the documents nonetheless continue to apply.

An exempt organization can make its application or a return *widely available* by posting the document on a World Wide Web page that the organization establishes and maintains. It can also satisfy the exception if the document is posted as part of a database of similar documents of other exempt organizations on a World Wide Web page established and maintained by another entity.

The document is considered widely available only if:

- The World Wide Web page through which it is available clearly informs readers that the document is available and provides instructions for downloading it.
- The document is posted in a format that, when accessed, downloaded, viewed, and printed in hard copy, exactly reproduces the image of the application or return as it was originally filed with the IRS, except for any information permitted by statute.
- Any individual with access to the Internet can access, download, view, and print the document without special computer hardware or software required for that format, and can do so without payment of a fee to the exempt organization or to another entity maintaining the World Wide Web page.

The organization maintaining the World Wide Web page must have procedures for ensuring the reliability and accuracy of the document that it posts on the page. It must take reasonable precautions to prevent alteration, destruction, or accidental loss of the document when printed on its page. If a posted document is altered, destroyed, or lost, the organization must correct or replace the document.[773]

---

[770] Reg. § 301.6104(d)-3(g).
[771] IRC §§ 6652(c)(1)(C), 6652(c)(1)(D), and 6685.
[772] Reg. § 301.6104(d)-4(a).
[773] Reg. § 301.6104(d)-4.

If the IRS determines that a tax-exempt organization is the subject of a *harassment campaign* and compliance with the requests that are part of the campaign would not be in the public interest, the organization is not required to fulfill a request for a copy that it reasonably believes is part of the campaign.

A group of requests for an organization's application or returns is indicative of a harassment campaign if the requests are part of a single coordinated effort to disrupt the operations of the organization, rather than to collect information about the organization. This is measured by a facts-and-circumstances test; factors include:

- A sudden increase in the number of requests
- An extraordinary number of requests made by means of form letters or similarly worded correspondence
- Evidence of a purpose to deter significantly the organization's employees or volunteers from pursuing the organization's exempt purpose
- Requests that contain language hostile to the organization
- Direct evidence of bad faith by organizers of the purported harassment campaign
- Evidence that the organization has already provided the requested documents to a member of the purported harassment group
- A demonstration by the tax-exempt organization that it routinely provides copies of its documents upon request

A tax-exempt organization may disregard any request for copies of all or part of any document beyond the first 2 received within any 30-day period or the first 4 received within any 1-year period from the same individual or the same address, irrespective of whether the IRS has determined that the organization is subject to a harassment campaign.

The regulations stipulate the procedure to follow for applying to the IRS for a determination that the organization is the subject of a harassment campaign. (There is no form.) The organization may suspend compliance with respect to the request, as long as the application is filed within 10 days after harassment is suspected, until the organization receives a response from the IRS.[774]

---

[774] Reg. § 301.6104(d)-5. There is one minor aspect of these regulations that one in a peevish mood might find annoying. This is based on the not unreasonable expectation that a government agency will make accurate reference, it its regulations, to a form over which it has administrative responsibility. The application an organization files with the IRS for a determination as to its tax-exempt status (Form 1023 or 1024) is termed an *application for recognition of exemption*. Despite the reference in these regulations, the term is not *application for tax exemption* (Reg. § 301.6104(d)-3(b)(3)(i)). If one's peevish mood persisted, one could get worked up to the point of believing that this is a deliberate attempt on the part of the IRS to perpetuate the myth that it has the power to grant tax-exempt status, when in fact its authority is confined to granting *recognition* of tax-exempt status (see *supra* § 6.7(a)).

# CHAPTER SEVEN

# Prospective Federal Regulation of Fund-Raising: Proposals and Issues

§ 7.4    The Prospective Federal Program Improvement Act

## § 7.4  THE PROSPECTIVE FEDERAL PROGRAM IMPROVEMENT ACT

p. 587, n. 56. *Replace "pp. 787-788" with "§ 24.5".*

p. 588, n. 58. *Replace "pp. 782-787" with "§ 24.4".*

# CHAPTER EIGHT

# Overviews, Perspectives, and Commentaries

## § 8.1 CHARITABLE FUND-RAISING AND THE LAW

### (f) Conclusion

p. 603, first paragraph of subsection. *In first line, replace "35" with "36".*

## § 8.2 DEFINING A FUND-RAISING PROFESSIONAL

p. 604, first paragraph of section. *In line 1, replace "48" with "49".*

## (a)  Definitions

p. 605, third paragraph. *In line 1, replace "34" with "35".*

## § 8.10   FUND-RAISING AND THE SUPREME COURT

p. 638, n. 173. *Insert following existing material:*

As of the close of the 1998 term, according to one analysis, the alignment in this regard of the Court has shifted over the years, so that Chief Justice Rehnquist now occupies the center of the Court, with the "liberals" being Justices Stephen G. Breyer, Ruth Bader Ginsburg, Souter, and John Paul Stevens, the "moderates" being Justices Kennedy, O'Connor, and Rehnquist, and the "conservatives" being Scalia and Thomas ("Supreme Court Weaves Legal Principles From a Tangle of Litigation," *New York Times*, June 30, 1998).

## § 8.12   THE IRS VIEW OF FUND-RAISING LAW IN THE 1990s

p. 644, n. 186. *Replace "Chapter 12" with "§ 4.6".*

p. 644, n. 187. *Replace "§ 13.7" with "§ 19.10".*

p. 645, n. 188. *Replace "Chapter 13" with "Chapter 19".*

## (b)  The Exclusivity Test

p. 646, n. 190. *Replace "Chapter 38" with "Chapter 25".*

## (f)  Meaning of the IRS Position

p. 653, lines 1-12. *Replace with:*

In a sense, the IRS position meant little in the absence of adoption by a court of some or all of its assertions. Nonetheless, however, this position illustrated how pervasive the IRS reach into the realm of charitable fund-raising can be, using the tests of exclusivity, private benefit, and private inurement. The IRS's stance in this regard could lead one to think that there is no need for enactment of a federal charitable solicitation act,[190.1] in that the elements of such a law are already in place.

As discussed,[190.2] the opinion of the trial court in this case was rendered and in fact the court adopted many of the assertions of the IRS. The court's decision was clearly articulated in relation to the rather bizarre facts of the case. At the same time, some rather broad principles were enunciated. The IRS now has the authority—which it had before, in any event—to review and consider the details of every contract between a charitable organization and a fund-raising individual or organization.

Before summarizing the court's opinion, here are the principles that may be gleaned from the

p. 654. *Replace carryover paragraph with*:

This brief of the U.S. government's position represents a sweeping application of basic federal tax law principles in a detailed and specific way to charitable fund-raising. Because the Tax Court did not address each of the government's 13 points, the opinion did not end up being as significant in the realm of fund-raising as it might have. (The heart of the case, from the standpoint of fund-raising, is in point 5.) Still, the opinion has much import in the fund-raising context, with a fund-raising company found to be an insider and the arrangement with a charity found to constitute private inurement. Additional cases of this nature may be anticipated.

## § 8.13  CHARITY AUCTIONS

### (e)  Quid Pro Quo Rules

p. 660, n. 222. *Replace sentence with:*

According to the tax regulations, a patron at a charity auction can rely on the charity's estimation of value of an item unless the patron knows or has reason to know that the estimate is unreasonable or is otherwise in error (Reg. § 1.170A-1(h)(4)(ii)).

[190.1] See Chapter 7.
[190.2] See *supra* § 6.15.

p. 666. *Insert new sections:*

## § 8.15A FUND-RAISING AND INTERMEDIATE SANCTIONS (NEW)

The long-awaited intermediate sanctions rules were signed into law on July 30, 1996.[245.1] This historic development brings into the federal tax law one of the most significant bodies of regulation affecting charitable organizations ever enacted. The potential impact of this new tax law regime is enormous. This is due in part to the general effective date for this legislation: September 14, 1995.

The new sanctions[245.2] are designed to curb abuses in the arena of private inurement using a mechanism other than revocation of the charitable organization's tax exemption. These sanctions are applicable with respect to all public charitable organizations[245.3] and tax-exempt social welfare organizations.[245.4] These two categories of organizations are termed *applicable tax-exempt organizations.*[245.5]

In the past, revocation of an offending charitable organization's tax-exempt status has not solved the problem: The person receiving the undue benefit continued to retain it and the beneficiaries of the charitable organization's program were the ones who were hurt in the aftermath of loss of exemption. Intermediate sanctions are *intermediate* in the sense that they will be imposed on directors, officers, key employees, or other types of disqualified persons who engage in inappropriate private transactions.

### (a) Intermediate Sanctions in General

The heart of this body of tax law is the *excess benefit transaction.* A transaction is an excess benefit transaction if an economic benefit is provided by an applicable tax-exempt organization directly or indirectly to or for the use of a disqualified person, if the value of the economic benefit provided exceeds the value of the consideration received by the exempt organization for providing the benefit.[245.6] The immediate focus of intermediate sanctions will be unrea-

---

[245.1] P.L. 104-168, 104th Cong., 2d Sess. (1996), 110 Stat. 1452.

[245.2] IRC § 4958.

[245.3] That is, organizations tax-exempt by reason of IRC § 501(c)(3) other than private foundations as defined in IRC § 509(a).

[245.4] That is, organizations that are tax-exempt by reason of IRC § 501(c)(4).

[245.5] IRC § 4958(e).

[245.6] IRC § 4958(c)(1)(A).

sonable compensation—when a person's level of compensation is deemed to be in excess of the value of the economic benefit derived by the organization from the person's services. In that regard, an economic benefit may not be treated as compensation for the performance of services unless the organization clearly indicated its intent to so treat the benefit.[245.7]

The concept of the excess benefit transaction includes any transaction in which the amount of any economic benefit provided to or for the use of a disqualified person is determined in whole or in part by the revenues of one or more activities of the organization, where the transaction is reflected in tax regulations and results in private inurement.[245.8]

A *disqualified person* is any person who was, at any time during the five-year period ending on the date of the transaction, in a position to exercise substantial influence over the affairs of the organization, as well as a member of the family of such an individual and certain controlled entities.[245.9]

A disqualified person who benefited from an excess benefit transaction is subject to an initial tax equal to 25 percent of the amount of the excess benefit.[245.10] Moreover, this person will be required to return the excess benefit amount to the tax-exempt organization. An *organization manager* (usually a director or officer) who participated in an excess benefit transaction, knowing that it was such a transaction, is subject to an initial tax of 10 percent of the excess benefit.[245.11] An additional tax may be imposed on a disqualified person when the initial tax was imposed and the appropriate correction of the excess benefit transaction did not occur; in this situation, the disqualified person is subject to a tax equal to 200 percent of the excess benefit involved.[245.12]

If a transaction creating a benefit was approved by an independent board, or an independent committee of the board, a presumption arises that the terms of the transaction are reasonable.[245.13] The burden of proof would then shift to the IRS, which would have to overcome (rebut) the presumption to prevail. This presumption may cause a restructuring of the boards of directors or trustees of many charitable organizations.

[245.7] *Id.*

[245.8] IRC § 4958(c)(2).

[245.9] IRC § 4958(f)(1).

[245.10] IRC § 4958(a)(1).

[245.11] IRC § 4958(a)(2).

[245.12] IRC § 4958(b).

[245.13] H.R. Rep. No. 104-506, 104th Cong., 2d Sess. (1996).

## (b) Applicability in Fund-Raising Context

The concept of the excess benefit transaction applies in the context of payments for fund-raising services.

One circumstance is when the recipient of the funds is an employee of the exempt organization. Another is when the person paid is an independent contractor, such as an outside fund-raising company. The sanctions apply to disqualified persons, which essentially is an individual or other person who is in a position to exercise substantial influence over the affairs of the organization. (In this regard, an opinion by the U.S. Tax Court is of considerable import, in that a fund-raising company was found to have unduly dominated the operations of a public charity.[245.14])

In many respects, the concept of the excess benefit transaction is based on existing law concerning private inurement. However, the statute expressly states that an excess benefit transaction also includes any transaction in which the amount of any economic benefit provided to a disqualified person is determined at least in part by the revenues of the organization.[245.15] These transactions are referenced in the legislative history of the intermediate sanctions as *revenue-sharing arrangements.*[245.16]

The IRS and the courts have determined that a variety of revenue-sharing arrangements do not constitute private inurement.[245.17] This includes arrangements in which the compensation of a person is ascertained, in whole or in part, on the basis of the value of contributions generated. The legislative history of the sanctions states that the IRS is not bound by these prior determinations when interpreting and applying intermediate sanctions.

## (c) Import of Proposed Regulations

The IRS, on July 30, 1998 (the second anniversary of the signing into law of the intermediate sanctions legislation), issued proposed regulations amplifying the rules concerning excess benefit transactions.[245.18]

The likelihood of an individual or a fund-raising company being a disqualified person with respect to a charitable organization is increased where the fund-raising person is being paid, in whole or in part, on the basis of the revenues of the charitable organization (commission-based or percentage-

---

[245.14] See *supra* § 8.12.

[245.15] See *supra* note 245.8.

[245.16] H.R. Rep. No. 104-506, *supra* note 245.13, at 56.

[245.17] See *supra* § 6.12.

[245.18] REG-246256-96.

based fund-raising, which can be a form of revenue-sharing arrangement). The proposed regulations state that facts and circumstances tending to show that a person has substantial influence over the affairs of an organization include the fact that the person's compensation is based on revenues derived from activities of the organization that the person controls.[245.19]

Another element of the proposed regulations that bears on fund-raising considerations is the rule that a person "who has managerial control over a discrete segment of an organization may nonetheless be in a position to exercise substantial influence over the affairs of the entire organization."[245.20] Thus, a fund-raising person need not control the charity as such to be a disqualified person. It is only required that the person control a "discrete segment" of the entity. This can happen, for example, in the context of fund-raising by means of sales of services or special event fund-raising.

The proposed regulations contain an illustration of this point.[245.21] A charity enters into a contract with a company that manages bingo games. Under the contract, the company agrees to provide all of the staff and equipment necessary to carry out a bingo operation one night per week. The charity is to be paid, by the company, a percentage of the revenue from this activity; the company is to retain the balance of the proceeds. The charity does not provide any goods or services in connection with the bingo operation, other than the use of its hall for the bingo games. The annual gross revenue earned from the bingo operation represents more than one half of the charity's total annual revenue.

By reason of these facts, the bingo management company is a disqualified person with respect to the charity. The company controls the bingo game activity—a "discrete segment" of the operations of the charity, because it has "full managerial authority" over the charity's principal source of income. The company's compensation is based on revenues from an activity it controls. Consequently, the company is in a position to exercise substantial influence over the affairs of the charity.

A separate example makes the point that those who control a fund-raising company can also be disqualified persons with respect to a charity.[245.22] In the illustration, the stock of the bingo game management company is wholly owned by an individual, who is actively involved in managing the company. This individual is a disqualified person with respect to the charity.

It is thus critical that a charity (and perhaps a social welfare organization) review its fund-raising contracts, including general management agree-

---

[245.19] Proposed (Prop.) Reg. § 53.4958-3(e)(2)(iii).

[245.20] Prop. Reg. § 53.4958-3(e)(1).

[245.21] Prop. Reg. § 53.4958-3(f), Example 3.

[245.22] Prop. Reg. § 53.4958-3(f), Example 4.

ments, to determine whether the other party to the contract is controlling a discrete segment of the organization and is therefore a disqualified person.

It needs to be noted that this element of the law leads only to the conclusion that the person is a disqualified one. It does not mean that an excess benefit transaction is involved. Nonetheless, that outcome can be different where the compensation arrangement is a revenue-sharing transaction, as discussed next.

In general, an excess benefit transaction is one where an economic benefit is provided by an applicable tax-exempt organization to a disqualified person, where the value of the benefit provided is in excess of the consideration received by the exempt organization. A simple example of this is an excessive fund-raising fee paid by a charitable organization to a fund-raising company that is a disqualified person.

However, another form of excess benefit transaction is the revenue-sharing transaction. This is, as noted, a transaction where the amount of an economic benefit provided to or for the use of a disqualified person is determined, in whole or part, by the revenues of one or more activities of the organization, where private inurement results.

The proposed regulations make the point that a revenue-sharing transaction may be an excess benefit transaction regardless of whether the economic benefit provided to the disqualified person exceeds the fair market value of the consideration provided to the exempt organization. This can be the case if, at any point, the transaction permits a disqualified person to receive additional compensation without providing proportional benefits that contribute to the accomplishment of the organization's exempt purposes.[245.23]

According to the proposed regulations, if this type of economic benefit is provided as compensation for services, the relevant facts and circumstances to take into account include the relationship between the size of the benefit provided and the quality and quantity of the services provided, as well as the ability of the party receiving the compensation to control the activities generating the revenues on which the compensation is based.[245.24]

An example in the proposed regulations shows how a revenue-sharing transaction is not necessarily an excess benefit transaction.[245.25] It concerns the manager of an investment portfolio of an applicable exempt organization. The manager and several other professional investment managers work exclusively for the organization in an office located in the organization's building. The manager's compensation consists of a flat base annual salary, health insurance, eligibility to participate in a retirement plan, and a bonus. This bonus is equal to a percentage of any increase in the value of the organization's portfolio over the year (net of expenses for investment management other than

---

[245.23] Prop. Reg. § 53.4958-5(a).

[245.24] *Id.*

[245.25] Prop. Reg. § 53.4958-5(d), Example 1.

the in-house managers' compensation). The bonus gives the manager an incentive to provide the highest-quality service in order to maximize benefits and minimize expenses to the organization.

In this illustration, the manager has a "measure of control" over the activities generating the revenues on which the bonus is based. At the same time, however, the manager can increase his or her compensation only if the organization also receives a proportional benefit. Under these facts, this revenue-based bonus arrangement, while a revenue-sharing transaction, is not an excess benefit transaction.

There is an example in the proposed regulations illustrating how a revenue-sharing arrangement can be an excess benefit transaction.[245.26] A public charity enters into a contract with a company that manages charitable gaming activities for charities. This company is, because of the contract, a disqualified person (insider) with respect to the charity. The company agrees to provide all of the staff and equipment necessary to carry out the gaming activities for the charity, and to pay the charity a percentage of the net profits (calculated as the gross revenue less rental for the equipment, wages for the staff, prizes for the winners, and other specified operating expenses). The company retains the balance of the proceeds, after payment of the expenses and the charity's share of the profits.

The company controls the activities generating the revenue on which its compensation is based. Because the company owns the equipment and employs the staff, it controls what the charity is charged, including the profit the company makes in that connection. Thus, the company controls the net revenues relative to the gross revenues from the gaming activity.

This example emphasizes the fact that the company is not provided with an appropriate incentive to maximize benefits and minimize costs to the charity. The company benefits whether the expenses are high and net revenues low or whether expenses are low and the net revenues high. By contrast, the charity suffers if expenses for the gaming operation are high and the net revenues are low. All of the gross revenues generated by the gaming operation belong to the charity. This arrangement allows a portion of these revenues to inure to the company. Under these facts, there is a revenue-sharing transaction, private inurement, and therefore an excess benefit transaction. In fact, the *entire amount* paid to this company is an excess benefit.

It is essential for charities (and social welfare organizations) to review their contractual obligations to determine if a revenue-sharing feature lurks in any of them. If there is a revenue-sharing arrangement, the facts and circumstances need to be explored to see if the organization is receiving a proportional benefit as the result of the arrangement and if there is private

---

[245.26] Prop. Reg. § 53.4958-5(d), Example 2.

inurement. If the corresponding benefit is lacking and there is private inurement, an excess benefit transaction is present.

## § 8.15B FUND-RAISING OVER THE INTERNET AND STATE LAW RESTRICTIONS (NEW)[245.27]

The Internet has greatly expanded the number of charitable organizations capable of carrying out multistate solicitation activities. Essentially, to reach potential donors in all of the states, an organization needs nothing more than a personal computer and an account with an Internet provider. Once established, the organization's charitable appeal can instantly be made available to the entire Internet community. The large national and international charities with the resources necessary to assure compliance with the various state regulatory regimes are thus no longer the only ones affected by state charitable solicitation laws. Instead, even the smallest organizations, operating on shoestring budgets, are beginning to tap the national contributions market. Thus, the new technology does indeed alter the nature of communication in the charitable solicitations context—it renders it inexpensive.

If those states asserting jurisdiction over Internet fund-raising are justified in doing so, the result will be that even the smallest organizations—too small to afford multistate solicitation efforts over the telephone or through the mail—will be required to register under numerous state charitable solicitation laws simply by virtue of utilizing the new communications technology to solicit contributions. If they do not (or cannot) assure state-law compliance, they will be forced to decide between risking legal action in a number of foreign states or refraining from speaking altogether. The question is whether, under this new mix of facts, those state laws impermissibly restrict speech protected under the First Amendment.

But there is another, more interesting, question that must first be addressed: From a legal perspective, should Internet fund-raising appeals be treated any differently solely because they take place on the Internet? That is, should communication over this new medium be treated as anything other than communication, for which there already is a rich regulatory scheme?

To determine whether the various state charitable solicitation regimes unduly intrude upon the protected speech interest in such solicitation, the existing regulatory framework must be applied to the new set of facts. The first step in this analysis is to ascertain whether the act of placing an appeal for funds in a document on a computer in one state can subject the organiza-

---

[245.27] This section is a summary of a paper by Paul E. Monaghan, Jr., Esq., Tyler Cooper & Alcorn, New Haven, Connecticut, titled "Charitable Solicitation Over the Internet and State Law Restrictions," prepared under the direction of Professor John Simon, Yale Law School (1996).

tion to the jurisdiction of a foreign state. There is as yet no law directly on this subject. However, although not entirely on point, one court opinion may shed some light on the matter.

A federal court of appeals, in 1996, had the opportunity to discuss the legal status of computer-borne communications in the First Amendment context. Two individuals ran an adult-oriented bulletin board service from their home in California. The site was accessible to others around the nation via modems and telephone lines.

Working with the local U.S. Attorney's office in Tennessee, a postal inspector purchased a membership in this bulletin board service and succeeded in downloading allegedly obscene images from the bulletin board. The U.S. Attorney's office filed criminal charges against these individuals for, among other things, transmitting obscenity over interstate telephone lines from their computer. By relatively conservative Memphis community standards, the images involved were found by a jury in fact to constitute obscenity; the couple was convicted.

On appeal, this federal appellate court affirmed the convictions, holding inter alia that the crime of "knowingly us[ing] a facility or means of interstate commerce for the purpose of distributing obscene materials" does not require proof that the defendants had specific knowledge of the destination of each transmittal at the time it occurred.[245.28] Of interest in the Internet context, in determining that the crime occurred in Tennessee, rather than in California, the court placed considerable weight on its finding that "substantial evidence introduced at trial demonstrated that the . . . [bulletin board service] was set up so members located in other jurisdictions could access and order [obscene] files which would then be instantaneously transmitted in interstate commerce."[245.29]

If the reasoning of this appellate court is followed by the state courts, it appears that communication via computer constitutes sufficient contact with the foreign state to subject the communicator to local law. Applied in the charitable solicitation context, then, the import of this court decision is clear: Soliciting funds over the Internet, where users download Web pages residing in foreign jurisdictions, in all likelihood will constitute sufficient contact to subject the organization to the jurisdiction of the foreign state, and therefore to the foreign charitable solicitation regime.

It must next be determined whether such interstate communication constitutes *solicitation* encompassed by the laws of the states. Though no definite answer can be divined from the language of any one statute, a brief survey of some state statutes strongly indicates that Internet solicitation will be held in many jurisdictions to be subject to regulation. For example, in one state,[245.30]

---

[245.28] *United States* v. *Thomas,* 74 F.3d 701 (6th Cir. 1996).
[245.29] *Id.* at 709.
[245.30] New York.

solicitation covered by the charitable solicitation act is defined as the making of a fund-raising request "through any medium," regardless of whether any contribution is received. In another state,[245.31] the charitable solicitation law applies to all "request[s] of any kind for a contribution." In another state,[245.32] the law embraces "each request for a contribution." The statutory scheme in another state[245.33] applies to "any request, plea, entreaty, demand or invitation, or attempt thereof, to give money or property, in connection with which ... any appeal is made for charitable purposes." In still another state,[245.34] the law applies to organizations "soliciting or collecting by agents or solicitors, upon ways or in any other public places within the commonwealth to which the public have a right of access."

Certainly, it is difficult to see how Internet fund-raising is not caught by any of these strikingly broad provisions. As currently written, then, the statutes of at least five states can easily be construed to reach Internet charitable fund-raising.

Indeed, it is likely that most, if not all, of the state charitable fund-raising regulation regimes may be so construed, and that those statutes that fail as currently written can be appropriately amended without much trouble. The question is whether these laws would pass constitutional law muster.

Though this is certainly a matter of interpretation, and at this point only conjecture is possible, it is this writer's conclusion that state laws which require foreign charitable organizations to register in their jurisdictions because of Internet fund-raising are unconstitutional to the extent that they chill the speech of the smaller organizations. It could not be more clear that charitable solicitation is protected speech under the First Amendment. Existing law supports the proposition that state laws may not discriminate against small and unpopular charities in the name of curbing charitable solicitation fraud. Though registration requirements have in the past been upheld as reasonable, these cases were decided at a time when the multistate fund-raising drive was the province of larger, more powerful organizations. Applied to the fund-raising realities of today, shaped in large part by the new communications technology, these laws can no longer be seen as unburdensome on the speech interests of smaller organizations. Because such laws put the small organization to the choice of running afoul of state regulatory requirements or refraining from making charitable solicitations on the Internet, those laws are overbroad and should be invalidated.

There has been talk for some time on certain of the nonprofit-related newsgroups and listservs about the form such a new regulatory system might take. In the Internet fund-raising context, discussion has focused on the bene-

---

[245.31] Arizona.
[245.32] Arkansas.
[245.33] California.
[245.34] Massachusetts.

fits and viability of implementing a new system of registration, to be conducted on the Internet. Ideally, this type of system would provide charitable organizations with the ability to meet all of the state regulatory requirements by placing certain information online with a central repository. The benefits of such a system would be manifold: Registration would be rendered simple and inexpensive for organizations wishing to solicit contributions on the Internet, regulatory bodies would enjoy easy access to the filings of organizations stationed in many states, and the public could quickly conduct preliminary research on organizations to which they may be interested in contributing.

The advent of the Internet has simply made the need for adoption of a universal charitable fund-raising regime more pressing. But it has done more: It has made uniform registration more feasible. By allowing citizens and regulators of any state to access information on a single computer housing the required filings, the Internet has removed the logistical barriers that previously would have made universal registration difficult or even impossible to implement.[245.35]

\* § 8.15C   FUND-RAISING AND THE PRIVATE
INUREMENT DOCTRINE (NEW)

As discussed,[245.36] the U.S. Court of Appeals for the Seventh Circuit has reversed the U.S. Tax Court, concluding that a fund-raising company was not an insider, for private inurement purposes,[245.37] with respect to the public charity known as the United Cancer Council (UCC).[245.38]

The facts of this case were summarized earlier. Basically, UCC was (it has since become bankrupt) a public charity, so recognized by the IRS in 1969. In 1984, UCC entered into a five-year direct-mail fund-raising contract with the company. While UCC received about $2.25 million as the result of the fund-raising, the company received more than $4 million in fees. The parties had co-ownership rights in UCC's mailing list.

The Tax Court held that UCC paid the fund-raising company excessive compensation, that the company exploited its rights over the list for its private gain, that the company was an insider with respect to UCC, and that this

---

[245.35] The state of affairs in these regards was characterized in this fashion: "Most state charity officials say that since there has been no outcry from donors, they are content at this point to uphold the libertarian ethos of the Internet and leave on-line fund raisers alone" (Demko, "On-Line Solicitors: Tangled Web," X *Chron. Of Phil.* (No. 7) 23, 24 (Jan. 29, 1998)).

[245.36] See § 6.15(e).

[245.37] See § 6.12.

[245.38] *United Cancer Council, Inc.* v. *Commissioner,* 165 F.3d 1173 (7th Cir. 1999).

relationship gave rise to private inurement. The court upheld the IRS's retroactive revocation of UCC's exempt status in 1990, to the date in 1984 when the contract began.

The Court of Appeals grounded its findings on the premise that the "Tax Court's classification of [the fund-raising company] as an insider of UCC was based on the fundraising contract."[245.39] That is, the focus was on the contract's terms. The Tax Court and the IRS were characterized as contending that the "contract was so advantageous to [the fund-raising company] and so disadvantageous to UCC that the charity must be deemed to have surrendered the control of its operations and earnings to the noncharitable enterprise that it had hired to raise money for it."[245.40]

The appellate court wrote that "[f]undraising has become a specialized professional activity and many charities hire specialists in it."[245.41] It continued: "If the charity's contract with the fundraiser makes the latter an insider, triggering the inurement clause of section 501(c)(3) and so destroying the charity's tax exemption, the charitable sector of the economy is in trouble."[245.42]

UCC's "sound judgment" in entering into the contract with the fundraising firm was questioned by the appellate court. The court wrote that UCC "drove (so far as the record shows) the best bargain that it could, but it was not a good bargain."[245.43] Nonetheless, the court continued, the private inurement proscription "is designed to prevent the siphoning of charitable receipts to insiders of the charity, not to empower the IRS to monitor the terms of arm's-length contracts made by charitable organizations with the firms that supply them with essential inputs, whether premises, paper, computers, legal advice, or fundraising services."[245.44] The Tax Court and IRS's position, wrote the court, "threatens to unsettle the charitable sector by empowering the IRS to yank a charity's tax exemption simply because the Service thinks its contract with its major fundraiser is too one-sided in favor of the fundraiser, even though the charity has not been found to have violated any duty of faithful and careful management that the law of nonprofit corporations may have laid upon it."[245.45]

The court said it could not find anything in the facts to support the "theory" that "W&H seized control of UCC and by doing so became an insider."[245.46] Said the Court: "There is nothing that corporate or agency law

---

[245.39] *Id.* at 1176.
[245.40] *Id.* at 1175.
[245.41] *Id.* at 1176.
[245.42] *Id.*
[245.43] *Id.* at 1178.
[245.44] *Id.* at 1176.
[245.45] *Id.* at 1179.
[245.46] *Id.* at 1178.

would recognize as control."[245.47] It wrote that the Tax Court used the word *control* "in a special sense not used elsewhere, so far as we can determine, in the law, including the federal tax law."[245.48] (The Tax Court defined an *insider* as a person who has "significant control over the [charitable] organization's activities."[245.49])

The appellate court concluded that "[t]here was no diversion of charitable revenues to an insider here, nothing that smacks of self-dealing, disloyalty, breach of fiduciary obligation or other misconduct of the type aimed at by a provision of law that forbids a charity to divert its earnings to members of the board or other insiders."[245.50]

The Seventh Circuit remanded this case to the Tax Court for consideration in light of the doctrine of private benefit. As to this remand, the court wrote that the "board of a charity has a duty of care . . . and a violation of that duty which involved the dissipation of the charity's assets might (we need not decide whether it would—we leave that issue to the Tax Court in the first instance) support a finding that the charity was conferring a private benefit, even if the contracting party did not control, or exercise undue influence over, the charity. This, for all we know, may be such a case."[245.51]

This opinion, as these things go, is quite extraordinary; it is wrong in so many ways, both procedurally and substantively. Regarding procedure, it is common for a federal appellate court opinion to begin by discussing the appropriate standard for the court's review. It is noteworthy that the Seventh circuit skipped this step in its *UCC* opinion.

Yet here is what this same court had to say on the subject in 1984: "The Tax Court's holding [that an organization was not entitled to exemption] must be sustained on appeal unless clearly erroneous."[245.52] The *UCC* case should also have been reviewed under the "clearly erroneous" standard.

The Seventh Circuit is not alone in adhering to this standard. Here is the Fifth Circuit: "A finding that a corporation is not operated exclusively for charitable purposes cannot be disturbed unless clearly erroneous."[245.53] Second Circuit: "We review the Tax Court decision [finding an organization not entitled to exemption] for clear error."[245.54] Ninth Circuit: "[The] factual finding [that an organization is operated for a substantial non-exempt purpose] [is] reviewable under the clearly erroneous standard."[245.55] D.C. Circuit:

---

[245.47] *Id.*

[245.48] *Id.*

[245.49] *United Cancer Council, Inc.* v. *Commissioner,* 109 T.C. 326, 388 (1997).

[245.50] *United Cancer Council, Inc.* v. *Commissioner, supra* note 245.38, at 1179.

[245.51] *Id.* at 1180.

[245.52] *Granzow* v. *Commissioner,* 739 F.2d 265 (7th Cir. 1984).

[245.53] *Nationalist Movement* v. *Commissioner,* 37 F.3d 216 (5th Cir. 1994).

[245.54] *Orange County Agricultural Society, Inc.* v. *Commissioner,* 893 F.2d 529 (2d Cir. 1990).

[245.55] *Church by Mail, Inc.* v. *Commissioner,* 765 F.2d 1387 (9th Cir. 1985).

"[O]ur review [of a denial of tax exemption] is on a clearly erroneous basis."[245.56]

It thus was outside the province of the Seventh Circuit to decide whether the Tax Court was right or wrong. The most it can do is determine if the Tax Court was clearly erroneous in its *UCC* decision. Certainly, right or wrong, the Tax Court's judgment in this case was not clearly erroneous.

As to substance, many in the nonprofit sector are being cheered by this finding that a fund-raising company was not functioning as an insider with respect to a charitable organization, for purposes of the private inurement proscription. Those who support this outcome do so because they like what the court said. Unfortunately, the court lacked the authority to say what it said and what it said does not have much to do with the facts of this case, which admittedly are extreme. Radical facts often give rise to radical decisions (which probably is one reason why the IRS litigated this one).

Everyone likes to win; no one likes to lose. This is certainly true in litigation. Here, the nonprofit sector won (at least in the short run) and the government lost. Yet there are wins and there are wins. Some wins rest on reason; they are correct outcomes. Indeed, most wins are in this category. Other wins, however, are flukes, oddball results that are not deserved. This opinion from the Seventh Circuit—this disappointing excuse for an appellate opinion, this rambling and nonsensical collection of paragraphs, this veritable parataxis—is of the oddball category. The court, in trying to help the nonprofit sector, distorted or strayed widely from the facts of the case and the applicable law.[245.57]

This appellate court, obviously, was fearful of the IRS. It sees the Service poised to run amok in this area, out to revoke the tax-exempt status of every charity that gets entangled in what in hindsight is a bad business deal. The IRS was viewed as "yanking" charitable exemptions for those who enter into "one-sided" contracts. The court mused that if the "charity's contract with the fundraiser makes the latter an insider, . . . the charitable sector of the economy is in trouble."[245.58]

An argument does not get any more disingenuous than that. The Tax Court never made any such statement. In fact, the Tax Court said: "We are not holding that an arm's-length arrangement that produces a poor result for an organization necessarily would cause the organization to lose its tax-exempt status."[245.59]

---

[245.56] *Fund for the Study of Economic Growth & Tax Reform* v. *Internal Revenue Service,* 98-2 U.S.T.C. ¶50,908 (D.C. Cir. 1998).

[245.57] Many individuals who are not lawyers, and thus are not versed in the niceties of what appellate court opinions are supposed to look like, are quite taken with the Seventh Circuit's opinion. One of these nonlawyers observed, articulating a view that is unassailable, that the opinion was written with *attitude*.

[245.58] *United Cancer Council, Inc.* v. *Commissioner, supra* note 245.38, at 1176.

[245.59] *United Cancer Council, Inc.* v. *Commissioner, supra* note 245.49, at 388.

The fact is that the Seventh Circuit's position rests on a false premise. It was wrong for it to write that the "Tax Court's classification of W&H as an insider of UCC was based on the fundraising contract."[245.60] Rather, the conclusion as to insider status was based on the actual relationship between the parties that arose as the consequence of the contract. The facts are crystal clear that the fund-raising company had UCC in its clutches and exploited the charity for its private ends. It is nothing short of unbelievable for this appellate court to sweepingly assert that this contract was an arm's-length one and regard it as typical of fund-raising contracts.[245.61]

In its anti-IRS diatribe, the Seventh Circuit faulted the IRS for being "ignorant" of contract law.[245.62] The reverse is true: the court is ignorant of the law of tax-exempt organizations. How else to explain the astoundingly erroneous statement that the Tax Court's use of the word *control* is "not used elsewhere, so far as we can determine, in the law, including federal tax law"?[245.63] To what extent did the court make a determination? It could have looked in the Internal Revenue Code, where the term *disqualified person*, as applied with respect to public charities like UCC, is defined as any person who was "in a position to exercise substantial influence over the affairs of the organization."[245.64] That is almost identical to the Tax Court's definition.

How about the assertion that "nothing [here] smacks of self-dealing"?[245.65] Again, a mere glance at the Code would have been enlightening to the court. Although the self-dealing rules do not apply in this case, it was the appellate court that brought them up. Self-dealing includes furnishing of services between a charity and a disqualified person, payment of compensation by a charity to a disqualified person, and use of the assets of a charity by or for the benefit of a disqualified person.[245.66] Contrary to the Seventh Circuit's belief, the facts in this case reflect rampant self-dealing (in the generic sense).

Now this case is to be resolved by application of the private benefit doctrine. This has amounted to quite a mess. The Seventh Circuit never really addressed the question of whether there was private inurement in this case; it essentially focused on the question of whether the fund-raising company was an insider in relation to UCC. If there was private inurement (and there was) and that inurement was not insubstantial (and it was not), how could there not be private benefit? (The Tax Court has previously held that all forms of pri-

---

[245.60] *United Cancer Council, Inc.* v. *Commissioner, supra* note 245.38 at 1176.

[245.61] See § 8.7.

[245.62] *United Cancer Council, Inc.* v. *Commissioner, supra* note 245.38, at 1177.

[245.63] *Id.* at 1178.

[245.64] IRC § 4958(f)(1)(A). See § 8.15A(a), text accompanied by note 245.9.

[245.65] *United Cancer Council, Inc.* v. *Commissioner, supra* note 245.38, at 1179.

[245.66] IRC § 4941(d)(1)

vate inurement are also forms of private benefit.[245.67] Perhaps the appellate court does not know that.)

There is very little law on the private benefit doctrine (a byproduct of the operational test, which stipulates that organizations, to be charitable, must principally engage in charitable activities[245.68]). The principal court opinion in the realm of the private benefit doctrine was wrongly decided.[245.69] It appears that the *UCC* case will bring some illumination of the reaches of the private benefit doctrine—because of the Seventh Circuit's opinion, itself being an embarrassingly wrong decision.

In short, the Seventh Circuit had the opportunity to nicely solidify the law in this area and interlace the private inurement doctrine with the excess benefit transaction rules. The court, by mischaracterizing the facts and mistating or overlooking law, wasted this opportunity and unnecessarily injected considerable confusion with respect to the matter of vendors as insiders.

---

[245.67] *American Campaign Academy* v. *Commissioner*, 92 T.C. 1053 (1989).

[245.68] Reg. § 1.501(c)(3)-1.

[245.69] The case concerned an otherwise tax-exempt school that trained individuals for careers as political campaign managers or consultants. The court was troubled by the fact that nearly all of the school's graduates became employed by or consultants to candidates of the Republican Party. To reason to the conclusion that the school could not be tax exempt, the court invented the dichotomy of *primary* private benefit and *secondary* private benefit. The beneficiaries of the primary private benefit were the school's students; the provision of benefits of this nature could not be a basis for denial of exemption because it was an exempt function. The beneficiaries of the secondary private benefit were the employers of the school's graduates—Republican Party candidates and entities. The latter category of beneficiaries was portrayed as a "select group" representing a "particular targeted private interest" (*American Campaign Academy* v. *Commissioner, supra* note 245.67, at 1074, 1076). The problem with this analysis is that every exempt school benefits persons, such as employers, on a "secondary" basis. For example, the senior partners of law firms enjoy, as the consequence of employing recent law school graduates as associates, far greater private benefit than that engendered by any school for political campaign professionals.

# CHAPTER NINE

# Standards Enforcement by Independent Agencies

## § 9.7   STANDARDS ENFORCEMENT

p. 685, n. 17, line 9. *Delete* "seeks" *and substitute* "sought".

p. 685, n. 17. *Insert at end of note:*

The case, however, was ultimately settled.

p. 690. *Add new section at end of chapter:*

## § 9.9   A WATCHDOG AGENCY'S RESPONSE TO COMMENTARY (NEW)

The foregoing commentary (Commentary) drew a response (Response) from the National Charities Information Bureau.[35] This Response, lightly edited to conform to the book's format, follows.

The Commentary on the "watchdog" agencies is disappointing, distressing, and dishonest.

---

[35] Letter to the author from James J. Bausch, President, National Charities Information Bureau, dated May 30, 1996.

It is disappointing to those who might have expected the even-handedness of [treatment of] law in the book. It is distressing to those who are concerned with the health of the charitable sector, who believe in openness and accountability, and who promote supporting as generously as possible charities that do what they say they do and meet donors' expectations. And it is ultimately dishonest—you knew what NCIB has been saying and doing, and clearly chose to ignore or misstate facts that did not fit your preconceptions.

You are entitled (without my or anyone's permission, of course) to express any opinion you wish about organizations such as NCIB and PAS but, in a book that purports to be a standard legal reference for those concerned with fund-raising, one might have hoped that the strangely nonconforming chapter on "watchdogs" had been more clearly labeled as opinion, rather than cloaked in lawyerly sounding, morally outraged phrasing. The low road traveled in high-falutin' language remains the low road.

You are so wrong in so many statements that I hardly know where to begin or end a commentary on what you have written. Let me, for the record, cite a few of the more blatant examples of your adherence to wrong opinion and incorrect fact.

It is stated: "In too many cases, an organization is, for example, rotated from a 'Meets Standards' listing to a 'Do Not Meet Standards' listing at the very same time it is notified of the change in status." That is an outright untruth. NCIB gives organizations prior notice of such a change in status and sends all organizations prepublication copies of new reports about them, along with an explanatory letter seeking their input. We state a future date on which we will make our new report available to the public if we do not hear back. If organizations perceive the time as too short, they may call us and seek an extension, which we always agree to, even if it is several weeks or even longer. During this waiting period, an organization is listed as "Report on Update" and is never "rotated" from a "Meets" to "Not" listing as you describe.

When it was written that "it is sad but true that the watchdog agencies, as a justification for their existence, must constantly portray the charitable sector in the darkest terms," you are again stating something you know to be untrue. That is an absurd statement. NCIB has clearly and strongly stated that "the great majority of charities do their work well and merit the generous support of contributors"—a statement we have made in several ways, consistently, in print and in speaking, over an extended period of time, including while the book was being prepared and well before it was published. You are the party with the dark paintbrush and preconceived vested interest here.

Outrage was professed in the Commentary that, in "an egregious lack of adherence to . . . principle," NCIB and PAS "take issue with the organization on a matter involving one or more accounting principles or reporting practices" after that organization has reported its finances in accordance with generally accepted accounting principles. Either the Commentary is based on a naive belief that GAAP guidance is precise, concrete, and all-satisfying, or it offers a new and definitive example of disingenuousness. If you become interested in factual candor at some future time, you may wish to begin your education about GAAP and other matters by reading Regina Herzlinger's article in the March–April issue of the *Harvard Business Review*, entitled "Can Public Trust in Nonprofits and Governments Be Restored?" You may also know of Professor Herzlinger as the senior author of *Financial Accounting and Management Control of Nonprofit Organizations*. Professor H. David Sherman's sidebar on "The Gaps in GAAP" might be enlightening to one who seeks enlightenment. The point is, as representatives of AICPA and FASB routinely state, that GAAP allows very wide interpretation, and any given interpretation may not satisfy all relevant perspectives. One can reasonably assume that an expert like you already knew all of this and deliberately chose to distort the picture by ignoring it.

The Commentary harps on my talk at the "Fund Raising and the Law" meeting in Washington. Yes, I did report what reliable polls indicate concerning public opinion about the trustworthiness, efficiency, and effectiveness of the philanthropic sector and specifically about fund-raisers. I did not make up the "statistics," nor did I think that playing ostrich as if people's opinions did not exist or did not matter was an appropriate exercise. I also did not think I was asked to give a pep talk—although I will freely admit that I might appropriately have put more positives into that particular presentation. My purpose was to encourage those attending the conference to adopt three courses of action: to conduct themselves professionally in accordance with such principles as those expressed in the "Donor Bill of Rights," to work hard to restore public confidence in sound charities and sound fund-raising, and to drum out of the profession those who consistently bring philanthropy and fund-raising into disrepute. If the effect of my words was "to depress everyone in the room," I did not succeed in my goal—although a reliable witness asserts that it was you, bad-mouthing my presentation after I left, who worked hard to convince the participants that they should be depressed. It is not a matter of either elephant guns or flyswatters, but of facing up to reality and building up the good will and credibility that philanthropy and fund-raising must have.

Finally, as I have previously informed you more than once, I personally do not subscribe to a "dark" picture of America's charities, nor would I lead an organization that did. I have devoted three decades of my life to this sector, and have been raising funds for most of that time. I firmly believe that fund-raising for charitable causes is a desirable means to a desirable end. I applaud it and those who do it properly and well—and I absolutely believe that is the overwhelming majority of those involved. I condemn the small minority whose actions sling mud on good practitioners and on our sector precisely because they injure contributors, charities, and all the good fund-raisers.

All these things you have known, but chose to ignore. Where, one wonders, in your definition of law, does such purposeful ignorance and misstatement as you have put forth become just plain distortion, dishonesty, and defamation? There is no need for you to try to respond, as the self-serving bias of any answer you might give is already abundantly clear.

Your readers surely hoped for more integrity and less pandering to personal prejudgments and special interests than you have shown. I write far more in sorrow than in anger at the serious disservice you have done to our sector.

## § 9.10  A REPLY TO THE RESPONSE (NEW)

By virtue of the Response, one is not confined to the watchdog agencies' reports on charitable organizations to glean examples of the literary devices they so often employ: the arrogant tone, misleading phraseology, innuendo, attention-shifting to irrelevant points, and emphasis on insignificant detail to either obscure or taint the big picture.

For arrogance, nothing can surpass the concession that commentators are entitled to express opinions on the watchdog agencies absent their prior consent. Concerns about fair process are dismissed as "lawyerly sounding" phrasing and "high-falutin'" language. The Response states that NCIB no longer rotates charities from one category to another without notice. That is a commendable development and it is nice that the organization no longer engages in the practice, but is a trivial point in relation to the vast panorama of due process violations routinely committed by the watchdog agencies.

The most casual comparison of the Commentary with the Response yields the fact that the latter wholly sidesteps the essence of the former. That is that (1) the watchdog agencies are self-appointed and self-styled; (2) they are accountable to no external authority or constituency; (3) they falsely portray themselves as "voluntary" agencies; (4) they are staffed by individuals who are not competent to make the conclusions they reach; (5) they wield enormous leverage over hapless charities (which often comply out of fear) because of the power of the watchdogs' ratings and reports; and (6) they have never been subject to any serious external scrutiny. The Response is silent across the board in these regards.

The one concrete example to be found in the Response is telling in two respects. This is the matter of application of generally accepted accounting principles (GAAP). There is no question that these principles are the subject of considerable interpretation. But it should be obvious that the place to begin in understanding and applying GAAP is the principles themselves and the interpretations by those who are professionally competent to interpret them, namely, certified public accountants. The bias of the NCIB in this regard is dramatically revealed when the Response states that, to understand GAAP, one must initially turn to sources that criticize the principles. The fact is that the watchdog agencies often do not like the conclusions mandated by GAAP, and thus they openly attach themselves to any source that denigrates them. The point of the Commentary was not that the watchdog agencies interpret GAAP; it was that they substitute their judgment for that of the professionals who possess the competence to interpret these principles.

Overall, a lawyer's concern for the procedural and substantive rights of charitable organizations caught up in the clutches of one or more of the watchdog agencies becomes characterized by the Response as pandering to "special interests." Over two decades of law practice, witnessing charities mistreated and miscast by these groups becomes "personal prejudgment" and "self-serving bias." And that is just the beginning: What to make of charges of "distortion, dishonesty, and defamation"? Probably the best approach is to simply accord these claims the credence they are due, as reflected in the fact that the source of them grandly asserts that a mere Commentary in one chapter of a book constitutes a "serious disservice" to the charitable sector. The sector is hardier than that, as evidenced by its ability to survive the pretensions of and material damages inflicted by the watchdog agencies.[36]

---

[36] It was observed in § 9.8 that the watchdog agencies often demonstrate outright bias against the charitable sector. A classic example of this prejudice against the sector was the reaction of the heads of the PAS and the NCIB to the court decision rendering several provisions of the Los Angeles city and county charitable solicitation ordinances unconstitutional (*Gospel Missions of America v. Bennett*, 951 F. Supp. 1429 (C.D. Cal. 1997)) (see §§ 5.3, 5.6, 5.7, and 5.11). The former said: "The reduction of such local government regulatory activities places more of a burden on the donor to check out charities on their [sic] own"; the latter said he was disappointed in the holding: "The donor has the right to know how his [or her] donation is used" (Craig, "Judge Strikes Down Key Parts of Los Angeles's Tough Rules for Charities," 9 *Chron. of Phil.* (No. 8) 25 (Feb. 6, 1997)). These views amply illustrate that the watchdog agencies champion unchecked government regulation of fund-raising by the sector even to the point of its serious damage (the charitable organization involved was unjustifiably raided by 40 county sheriffs, and subjected to search and seizure at gunpoint)—irrespective of whether the law is egregiously unconstitutional. In the case, the court found 15 provisions of the ordinances to be unconstitutional on their face in violation of free speech rights, 6 provisions to be unconstitutional because of the unbridled discretion vested in government officials, and 5 provisions to be unconstitutional for various other reasons, including vagueness and violation of the Constitution's establishment clause! It is shameful that the watchdog agencies champion this type of law.

This antipathy against the sector was revealed in another context—this time in the aftermath of publication by the accounting profession of new rules concerning joint cost allocations (Statement of Position 98-2, published by the American Institute of Certified Public Accountants as an adjustment to rules written in 1987). Many charity officials have objected to these rules, finding them to be "too strict and . . . biased against legitimate fund-raising activities" (Billitteri and Blum, "Unsettled Accounts," X *Chron. of Phil.* (No. 11) 41 (Mar. 26, 1998)). Predictably, the principal watchdog agencies decided that the "revised policy is too lenient, allowing charities to hide some fund-raising costs in other accounting categories" (*id.*). Thus, while one of the nation's premier accountants in the nonprofit field (who participated in the writing of the Statement), Richard Larkin, said that the "underlying concept" of the 1998 rules "is still the same" as that of the 1987 rules, and that the "difference is only in the details," the president of the NCIB said: "The bottom line is that contributors deserve better" (*id.* at 42).

# APPENDIX G

# INFLATION-ADJUSTED INSUBSTANTIALITY THRESHOLD—$50 TEST

| Year | Amount | Rev. Proc. |
| --- | --- | --- |
| 1993 | $62.00 | 92-102, 1992-2 C.B. 579 |
| 1994 | 64.00 | 93-49, 1993-2 C.B. 581 |
| 1995 | 66.00 | 94-72, 1994-2 C.B. 811 |
| 1996 | 67.00 | 95-53, 1995-2 C.B. 445 |
| 1997 | 69.00 | 96-59, 1996-2 C.B. 390 |
| * 1998 | 71.00 | 97-57, 1997-2 C.B. 584 |
| * 1999 | 72.00 | 98-61, 1998-52 I.R.B. 18 |

# APPENDIX H

# INFLATION-ADJUSTED INSUBSTANTIALITY THRESHOLD—$25 TEST

| Year | Amount | Rev. Proc. |
|------|--------|------------|
| 1991 | $28.58 | 92-58, 1992-2 C.B. 410 |
| 1992 | 30.09 | 92-58, 1992-2 C.B. 410 |
| 1993 | 31.00 | 92-102, 1992-2 C.B. 579 |
| 1994 | 32.00 | 93-49, 1993-2 C.B. 581 |
| 1995 | 33.00 | 94-72, 1994-2 C.B. 811 |
| 1996 | 33.50 | 95-53, 1995-2 C.B. 445 |
| 1997 | 34.50 | 96-59, 1996-2 C.B. 390 |
| * 1998 | 35.50 | 97-57, 1997-2 C.B. 584 |
| * 1999 | 36.00 | 98-61, 1998-52 I.R.B. 18 |

# A P P E N D I X   I

## INFLATION-ADJUSTED
## LOW-COST ARTICLE DEFINITION

| Year | Amount | Rev. Proc. |
|---|---|---|
| 1991 | $5.71 | 92-58, 1992-2 C.B. 410 |
| 1992 | 6.01 | 92-58, 1992-2 C.B. 410 |
| 1993 | 6.20 | 92-102, 1992-2 C.B. 579 |
| 1994 | 6.40 | 93-49, 1993-2 C.B. 581 |
| 1995 | 6.60 | 94-72, 1994-2 C.B. 811 |
| 1996 | 6.70 | 95-53, 1995-2 C.B. 445 |
| 1997 | 6.90 | 96-59, 1996-2 C.B. 390 |
| * 1998 | 7.10 | 97-57, 1997-2 C.B. 584 |
| * 1999 | 7.20 | 98-61, 1998-52 I.R.B. 18 |

## APPENDIX J

# STANDARDIZED REGISTRATION FOR NONPROFIT ORGANIZATIONS UNDER STATE CHARITABLE SOLICITATION LAWS

A product of an ongoing project of the
National Association of Attorneys General (NAAG)
and the National Association of
State Charities Officials (NASCO)

ver. 2.10 April, 1999

## Introduction & Contents

**Why must my organization "register?"**

The simple answer is: it's the law. Typically, states exercise regulatory authority over nonprofits based on one (or both) of two premises: the nonprofit is physically "present" in the state (e.g., has an office, owns real estate, or conducts program activities) *or* the nonprofit raises funds in the state.

In either case, a state might require the nonprofit to "register," that is, to provide identifying information about the nonprofit and its operations. It is the latter premise for registration—raising funds—that provides the impetus for the Unified Registration Statement (and the movement for standardized reporting in general). Organizations of *any* size and *any* means may find that raising funds from the public—even when conducted modestly from a single location—will give rise to multiple regulatory obligations.

In fact, today *most* states regulate fundraising. They do so through statutes—usually called "solicitation laws"—which are primarily concerned with the solicitation of charitable contributions from the general public. The centerpiece of most of the regulatory schemes is comprehensive reporting, by nonprofits and by the outside fundraising firms and consultants they employ.

## What is "registration?"

Compliance reporting under solicitation laws is divided into two pieces: (1) *registration,* which provides an initial base of data and information about an organization's finances and governance and (2) *annual financial reporting,* which keeps the states apprised about the organization's operations, with the emphasis on fundraising results and practices. Typically, states require *both* registration (at least an initial registration) and annual financial reporting.

With approximately forty states regulating in this manner, there is inevitably little consistency of approach. Some states have one-time registration; others require annual renewal of registration; some will require submission of every common governance and financial document; others make do with just an IRS Form 990; and so forth. But each has its own registration form (or forms) and, until the advent of the URS, required its submission, verbatim.

PLEASE TAKE SPECIAL NOTE: The URS and this packet address *registration* only. *The URS can not be used to fulfill annual financial reporting requirements.* A separate project to produce a standardized format, like the URS, is under way (see below). For now, the URS is the sole device for standardized, multi-state filing and it applies *only* to registration and registration renewal (which may be required yearly but, we say again, should not be confused with annual financial reporting).

## Which nonprofits must register (and when)?

Generally, any nonprofit that conducts a charitable solicitation within the borders of a state, *by any means,* is subject to its law and is therefore required to register. Also generally, the operative terms "charitable" and "solicitation" are defined very broadly and may even include, for example, an Internet posting by an environmental organization inviting contributions from the public.

In other words, the soliciting organization need not be a "charity" in the strict sense nor have any physical presence of any kind in the state. So, a letter, phone call or newspaper ad requesting financial support from a state's residents is enough, in the unchallenged legal opinion of the states, to trigger the coverage of that state's solicitation law.

Against this framework of all-inclusiveness is a patchwork of *exclusions from coverage*. These are the product of each state's constitutional and political considerations. So, either through exemption from registration requirements or out-and-out exclusion from the law, each state excuses some nonprofits from registering. For example, every state grants an exemption (or exclusion) to "religious organizations," as the term is respectively defined, and most have exemptions for colleges and universities or for organizations raising only small amounts (say, under $5,000). See the Appendix for details.

Significantly, technical compliance with any state's registration law requires initial registration *before* the first solicitation has been directed into the state. But the fact remains that many nonprofits have not done the necessary legal homework before launching their fundraising campaigns. If your nonprofit is one of these, you should be concerned—very concerned. But you *should not be deterred* from going ahead with registration because you fear that you're a lawbreaker already and it's too late.

Failure to register before soliciting *is* a violation of law and *could* subject the organization (and in some circumstances, its officers or directors) to whatever sanctions (e.g., a substantial fine) exist in each state's law. But, the states generally wish to encourage honest efforts to comply with registration laws and tend to employ sanctions only when enforcement officials deem it necessary. So, an organization that can demonstrate its good faith and promptly registers after discovering its obligation (albeit tardily) stands a good chance of avoiding or minimizing sanctions. The bottom line: registrations is the law and you should comply as soon as possible.

## What is the Unified Registration Statement?

The URS represents an effort to consolidate the information and data requirements of all states requiring registration. The effort, organized by the National Association of State Charities Officials and the National Association of Attorneys General, is one part of an ongoing project whose aim is to standardize, simplify, and economize compliance under the states' solicitation laws.

The effort consists of three phases: (1) compile an inventory of registration information demands from *all* states, (2) produce a format (or form) which incorporates all (or most) of these demands, and (3) encourage the states to accept this "standardized" format as an alternative to their own forms. The effort is dynamic and ongoing, now represented by version 2.10 of the URS which is accepted by thirty-three of the thirty-nine jurisdictions requiring registration. Reflecting this dynamic, *the URS will be updated continually* by way of its website *(http://www.nonprofits.org/library/gov/urs/)*. See Item #6 in the "Reminders" section (URS Instructions, pg 4) for more information on URS packet updates.

### How do you use the URS?

The URS is an *alternative* to the respective registration forms produced by the cooperating states. In those states, a registering nonprofit may use *either* the state form or the URS. It follows that the URS will prove most useful to those nonprofits who are soliciting regionally or nationally and who are therefore subject to the registration laws of *multiple* states. But the URS may be used by any nonprofit which is registering in a state accepting it.

Conceptually, the process is simple: fill out the URS by following its accompanying instructions, photocopy the completed URS (with state-specific items, including signature lines, left blank), fill in any state specific items, execute (i.e., signing or notarized signing) according to each state's requirements, collect and attach the specified governance (for initial filings) and other documents, write a check for the prescribed registration fee (if any), and mail the package, covered by the URS, to the respective state's administering agency (See Appendix).

### What's in this packet?

The URS is presented here along with additional materials and information. The goal is to enable many, if not most, users to complete their registrations (for URS states) without the need to acquire information or materials outside this packet. Please read the following description of the packet's contents to learn what's here and where to find it:

- *URS* (3 pgs) and *Instructions* (4 pgs) - Only one copy of the URS is provided with this packet. Make a back up photocopy of the blank form before you begin work. Also, note that the submitted URS will be considerably longer than the 3 pages of the form since several of the 22 URS information items require attached lists.
- *Supplementary Forms* (8 forms from 6 jurisdictions) - A number of states wished to cooperate with the URS effort but found it necessary for legal or other reasons to request information and/or offer instruction on forms designed to supplement the URS. For those states, the URS must be accompanied by the respective supplementary form or information.

- *Appendix* (13 pgs) - Provides state-by-state filing details for each of the thirty-three cooperating states. Please closely attend to the following notes for helpful information about the Appendix:

  (1)  The *Exemptions* entries are NOT verbatim from the laws. If you believe that your organization is exempt in one or more states, be cautious and refer to the law (See *Governing law* in the Appendix for citation), regulations and/or applicable form from each respective state.

  (2)  *Due Date* refers to the day that registration renewals are due. See below for information on due dates for annual financial reports.

  (3)  *FR Contracts* refers to the actual contractual documents establishing your relationship with outside fundraising professionals described in URS Item 20. A "yes" here in a state's entry means that you must copy and submit all such contracts along with the URS, for that state. Note too that subsequent contracts may have to be submitted (either when entered into, with registration renewal, or as part of required annual financial reporting).

  (4)  Your *Certificate of Incorporation, Bylaws,* and *IRS Determination Letter* (official letter from Internal Revenue Service establishing your federal tax-exempt status) are all one-time submissions with initial registration. Unless amended after the initial registration, they need not accompany renewal filings.

  (5)  In obvious contrast, *Audit* and *IRS Form 990* change from year to year. A "yes" means that the most recent completed versions must be submitted with the URS. Note too that while a state (e.g., Oregon) may not require either for purposes of registration, it might require the current version of either or both as part of annual financial reporting.

  (6)  *States not yet accepting the URS* are listed in a separate section. Included are contacts for registration information.

  (7)  Basic *information on annual financial reporting* for all URS states is included in a separate section. Although the URS cannot be used to fulfill annual financial reporting requirements, the information is provided here to help filers understand and coordinate their reporting obligations.

- *Helps* (3 pgs) - provides several aids for filers, itemized below:

  (1)  *Checklist* - recapitulates much of the Appendix in an easy-to-read, yes-no format. It will serve as a useful tool when, for example, you are submitting multiple registrations and need to be assured that each state's stack has the necessary components.

  (2)  *Changes to the URS* - a cumulative listing of changes made to v. 2.00 of the URS packet.

  (3)  *Site List* - sources for copies of the URS.

**APPENDIX J**

**What's next for the Standardized Reporting Project?**

In every sense, both the URS and the Project are a work in progress. There are four components to reporting under the solicitation laws: registration for nonprofits, annual reporting for nonprofits, registration for outside professionals and annual reporting for outside professionals. Though work on other of the four components is under way, the URS (nonprofit registration) is the sole product in service.

And while the "standardized" approach implies continual change, even the threshold work on the URS is not complete. For example, page 11 of the Appendix lists the few remaining states which, for one reason or another, have not yet chosen to participate by accepting the URS. Neither the URS nor any subsequent products will achieve maximum utility until *all states* are cooperating.

This version 2.10 of the URS packet contains numerous refinements, many of them the product of user comments. Consequently, your feedback is very important. Please direct any comments you may have about suggested improvements (or about errors you believe you've discovered) to the URS and its instructions, or to the accompanying materials to:

| | | |
|---|---|---|
| Karin K. Goldman | and/or | Leith R. Alvaro |
| Asst. Attorney General | | Staff Attorney |
| Charities Bureau | | Multi-State Filer Program |
| Office of the Attorney General | | 1612 K Street NW #510 |
| 120 Broadway 3rd Floor | | Washington, DC 20006-2802 |
| New York, NY 10271-0002 | | |

# STANDARDIZED REGISTRATION FOR NONPROFITS

## Unified Registration Statement (URS) for Charitable Organizations (v. 2.10)

☐ **Initial registration**    ☐ **Renewal/Update**

This URS covers the reporting year which ended (day/month/year) _____

Filer EIN _____

State _____    State ID _____

1. Organization's legal name _____

   If changed since prior filings, previous name used _____

   All other name(s) used _____

2 (A). Street address _____

   City _____    County _____

   State _____    Zip Code _____

   (B). Mailing address (if different) _____

   City _____    County _____

   State _____    Zip Code _____

3. Telephone number (s) _____    Fax number (s) _____

   E-mail _____    Web site _____

4. Names, addresses (Street & P.O.), telephone numbers of other offices/chapters/branches/affiliates (attach list).

5. Date incorporated _____    State of incorporation _____

   Fiscal year end: day/month _____

6. If not incorporated, type of organization, state and date established _____

   _____

7. Has organization or any of its officers, directors, employees or fund raisers:

   A. Been enjoined or otherwise prohibited by a government agency/court from soliciting?    Yes ☐    No ☐

   B. Had its registration been denied or revoked?    Yes ☐    No ☐

   C. Been the subject of a proceeding regarding any solicitation or registration?    Yes ☐    No ☐

   D. Entered into a voluntary agreement of compliance with any government agency or in a case before a court or administrative agency?    Yes ☐    No ☐

   E. Applied for registration or exemption from registration (but not yet completed or obtained?    Yes ☐    No ☐

   F. Registered with or obtained exemption from any state or agency?    Yes ☐    No ☐

   G. Solicited funds in any state?    Yes ☐    No ☐

   If "yes" to 7A, B, C, D, E, *attach explanation.*

   If "yes" to 7F & G, *attach list* of states where registered, exempted or where it solicited, including registering agency, dates of registration, registration numbers, any other names under which the organization was/is registered, and the dates and type (mail, telephone, door to door, special events, etc.) of the solicitation conducted.

8. Has the organization applied for or been granted IRS tax exempt status?    Yes ☐    No ☐

   If yes, date of application _____ OR date of determination letter _____.

   If granted, exempt under 501(c) _____.    Are contributions to the organization tax deductible?    Yes ☐    No ☐

# APPENDIX J

9. Has tax exempt status ever been denied, revoked or modified?   Yes ☐   No ☐

10. Indicate all methods of solicitations:

    Mail ☐   Telephone ☐   Personal Contact ☐   Radio/TV Appeals ☐
    Special Events ☐   Newspaper/magazine ads ☐   Other(s) ☐ (specify) _____

11. List the NTEE code(s) that best describes your organization   _____, _____, _____

12. Describe the purposes and programs of the organization and those for which funds are solicited (*attach separate sheet if necessary*).

    _____
    _____
    _____
    _____

13. List the names, titles, addresses (Street & P.O.), and telephone numbers of officers, directors, trustees, and the principal salaried executives of organization (*attach separate sheet*).

14 (A) (1). Are any of the organization's officers, directors, trustees or employees related by blood, marriage, or adoption to: (i) any other officer, director, trustee or employee OR (ii) any officer, agent, or employee of any fundraising professional firm under contract to the organization OR (iii) any officer, agent, or employee of a supplier or vendor firm providing goods or services to the organization?   Yes ☐   No ☐

   (2). Does the organization or any of its officers, directors, employees, or anyone holding a financial interest in the organization have a financial interest in a business described in (ii) or (iii) above OR serve as an officer, director, partner or employee of a business described in (ii) or (iii) above?   Yes ☐   No ☐
   (If yes to any part of 14A, *attach sheet* which specifies the relationship and provides the names, businesses, and addresses of the related parties).

   (B). Have any of the organization's officers, directors, or principal executives been convicted of a misdemeanor or felony? (*If yes, attach a complete explanation.*)   Yes ☐   No ☐

15. *Attach separate sheet listing names and addresses (street & P.O.) for all below:*

    Individual(s) responsible for custody of funds.         Individual(s) responsible for distribution of funds.

    Individual(s) responsible for fund raising.             Individual(s) responsible for custody of financial records.

    Individual(s) authorized to sign checks.                Bank(s) in which registrant's funds are deposited (*include account number and bank phone number*).

16. Name, Address (Street & P.O.), and telephone number of accountant/auditor.

    Name _____
    Address _____
    City _____ State _____ Zip Code _____ Telephone _____
    Method of accounting _____

17. Name, address (Street & P.O.), and telephone number of person authorized to receive service of process. *This is a state-specific item. See instructions.*

    Name _____
    Address _____
    City _____ State _____ Zip Code _____ Telephone _____

# STANDARDIZED REGISTRATION FOR NONPROFITS

18 (A). Does the organization receive financial support from other non-profit organizations (foundations, public charities, combined campaigns, etc.)?   Yes ☐  No ☐

   (B). Does the organization share revenue or governance with any other non-profit organization?   Yes ☐  No ☐

   (C). Does any other person or organization own a 10% or greater interest in your organization OR does your organization own a 10% or greater interest in any other organization?   Yes ☐  No ☐

   (If "yes" to A, B or C, *attach an explanation* including name of person or organization, address, relationship to your organization, and type of organization.)

19. Does the organization use volunteers to solicit directly?   Yes ☐  No ☐

   Does the organization use professionals to solicit directly?   Yes ☐  No ☐

20. If your organization contracts with or otherwise engages the services of any outside fundraising professional (such as a "professional fundraiser," "paid solicitor," "fund raising counsel," or "commercial co-venturer"), *attach list* including their names, addresses (street & P.O.), telephone numbers, and location of offices used by them to perform work on behalf of your organization. Each entry *must include* a simple statement of services provided, description of compensation arrangement, dates of contract, date of campaign/event, whether the professional solicits on your behalf, and whether the professional at any time has custody or control of donations.

21. Amount paid to PFR/PS/FRC during previous year: $ _____

22 (A). Contributions in previous year: $ _____

   (B). Fundraising cost in previous year: $ _____

   (C). Management & general costs in previous year: $ _____

   (D). Fundraising costs as a percentage of funds raised: _____

   (E). Fundraising costs plus management & general costs as a percentage of funds raised: _____

---

**Under penalty of perjury, we certify that the above information and the information contained in any attachments is true, correct, and complete.**

Sworn to before me on (or signed on) _____, 19 _____

_____
Notary public (if required)

_____          _____
Name (printed)                                              Name (printed)

_____          _____
Name (signature)                                           Name (signature)

_____          _____
Title (printed)                                                Title (printed)

---

**Consult the state-by-state appendix to the URS to determine whether supporting documents, supplementary state forms or fees must accompany this form. Before submitting your registration, *make sure you have attached or included everything required by each state to the respective copy of the URS.***

**Attachments may be prepared as one continuous document or as separate pages for each item requiring elaboration. In either case, please number the response to correspond with the URS item number.**

■  129  ■

# INSTRUCTIONS for Unified Registration Statement (URS)

[Preliminary identifying information: Indicate whether registration is **initial** or **renewal** by checking the correct box at top of page; Insert state-specific end date for registration period covered by this URS—applicable to renewals and to states with a fixed-date reporting cycle ("N/A" as to states with one-time registration. Leave blank for initial registration in states with "anniversary" due dates.); Fill in your organization's federal Employer Identification Number (EIN); Enter state to which *this particular copy* of the URS will be submitted; Enter state-specific ID in the space provided if this is a renewal or update and the state to which *this particular copy* of the URS will be submitted has assigned your organization a unique file, license or identifying number]

Item #1: Enter organization's legal name; previous name used if an immediately prior filing was made under the previous name; and any other names the organization may be identified as or known as. Under "other names", include any distinctive names, such as one given to a particular campaign, the organization uses for purposes of public solicitation (e.g., "The Citywide Dance Project" of Houston Arts Advocates, Inc).

Item #2(A,B): Fill out complete street address in item #2A. Fill out complete **mailing** address (e.g., a generally used PO box) in item #2B, if different from above.

Item #3: List primary telephone and facsimile numbers. Also, provide address for electronic mail or web site(s) if used to provide information to or to communicate with the public.

Item #4: Attach list of all other offices, chapters, branches and/or affiliates with complete names and addresses. PLEASE NOTE that Kansas, Maine, Mississippi, and Tennessee require that you specifically indicate the offices, chapters, etc. for their states in your respective URS submission to them.

Item #5: Fill out organization's date of incorporation, the state where it was incorporated and the day and month of its fiscal year end. Got to Item #7.

Item #6: **If your organization is not incorporated,** list the type of organization, state in which it is located, and date of establishment (if a partnership, include the partners' names, addresses and telephone numbers).

Item #7: Answer questions A through G by checking the appropriate box. If you answer "yes" to A, B, C, D and/or E, you **must** attach a written explanation. If you answer "yes" to F and/or G, attach a listing of all states where *registered* or from whom an *exemption* was obtained or in which your organization *solicited* contributions (include agencies, dates of registration, registration numbers, any other names organization was/is registered under, and the dates and types of solicitation conducted).

**VERY IMPORTANT**: In answering 7G for an **initial registration** in a given state, make sure that you have provided a specific date when solicitation began (if your answer to 7G is "yes") in that state; OR, if your answer to 7G is "no" (or "no" as to the state in question) but you *intend to begin* soliciting, give the approximate date you expect to begin soliciting in that state.

Item #8: Answer by checking appropriate box. If you answer "yes," list date of application or the date of the IRS determination letter. If exempt status has been granted, supply the IRS Code section number (e.g., "501(c)(*3*)" or "501(c)(*4*)") under which the organization secured its exemption. *Please note* that some states also require a copy of the organization's IRS determination letter or application for exemption (see state-by-state Appendix).

Item #9: Answer by checking appropriate box. If you answer "yes," please attach a written explanation.

Item #10: Answer by checking all appropriate boxes. Use blank to specify any solicitation method not listed (if your organization raises funds by *operating or sponsoring games of chance,* such as *bingo* or *"casino nights"*, you must report that fact, specifying the game, in the "Other" blank).

Item #11: The National Taxonomy of Exempt Entities (NTEE) is a system for classifying nonprofits developed by the National Center for Charitable Statistics. From the twenty-six major groupings of the NTEE system, below, select the code letter that best describes your organization's primary purpose or field (you may enter a second or third code letter if no single code seems adequate):

A    Arts, Culture, Humanities
B    Educational institutions & Related activities
C    Environmental Quality, Protection & Beautification
D    Animal related
E    Health-general & rehabilitative
F    Mental health, Crisis intervention
G    Disease, Disorders, Medical disciplines
H    Medical research
I    Crime, Legal related
J    Employment, Job related
K    Food, Nutrition, Agriculture
L    Housing, Shelter

M   Public safety, Disaster preparedness & relief
N   Recreation, Sports, Leisure, Athletics
O   Youth development
P   Human services
Q   International, Foreign affairs, National security
R   Civil rights, Social action, Advocacy
S   Community improvement, Capacity building
T   Philanthropy, Voluntarism and Grantmaking foundations
U   Science and Technology research
V   Social Science research
W   Public affairs, Society benefit
X   Religion, Spiritual development
Y   Mutual/membership benefit
Z   Unknown, unclassifiable

<u>Item #12</u>: Explain purposes and programs of organization for which funds are solicited. If programs are directed to specific beneficiaries, list or describe the beneficiaries. Attach a separate sheet of paper if necessary.

<u>Item #13</u>: Attach list of officers, directors and executives or organization complete with their *residence* addresses and telephone numbers. At your discretion, you may supply a *daytime* phone number instead, so long as the person can generally be reached at that number during normal business hours.

<u>Item #14</u>: (A)(1&2) Answer by checking appropriate box. If you answer "yes" to any of the relationships described, attach the requested information for *all* the related parties.

    (B) Answer by checking appropriate box. If you answer "yes," attach a written explanation. A "misdemeanor or felony" is a crime and *does not include* violations of civil ordinances, such as minor traffic offenses.

<u>Item #15</u>: On an attached sheet, provide the names and addresses of the people with the specified responsibilities. Please clearly indicate the respective responsibility for each name listed. Also include the names, addresses, and phone numbers of all banks, *and all accounts* (provide numbers), in which organization's funds are deposited. "Custody" means legal custody of the organization's funds, typically the charge of the Treasurer. Person responsible for "distribution" means the person, typically the President or chief executive, who has primary day-to-day authority over disposing of the organization's funds.

<u>Item #16</u>: List name, address and telephone number of organization's outside accountant and/or auditor. Exclude from this item an outside accountant or accounting firm employed solely as a bookkeeper.

<u>Item #17</u>: This item should be left blank, expect for a few selected instances, specified below. Some states require that you appoint one of their residents to receive legal notices ("service of process") in order to effect your registration. This person is variously termed a "resident agent" or "registered agent." Of the states that require such an appointment, some permit you to make it by filling in this item on the URS. Fill in this item **only for each such state,** and then, only with the name, address and telephone number of the agent for *that* state. Consult the state-by-state Appendix for further information.

<u>Item #18</u>: Answer by checking appropriate box. Provide all the requested information for all persons or organizations producing a "yes" (and if yes for 18C, specify the percentage interest). For "type of organization", include both organizational structure (such as "corporation", partnership", or "unincorporated association") and whether the organization is for-profit or nonprofit.

<u>Item #19</u>: Answer by checking the appropriate box. A person solicits "directly" when they have actual contact with potential donors, such as when placing telephone calls or when going door-to-door.

<u>Item #20</u>: Attach listing of the outside professionals that provide fundraising services to your organization. Include in the list companies who are conducting "cause-related marketing" for your benefit (such companies are subject to regulation—typically as "commercial co-venturers"—under the solicitation laws of several states). Supply a complete address (street & PO) and phone number for each office location providing services.

The terms employed (e.g., "fund raising counsel"), although commonly used, are illustrative only. In practice, the precise and operative definitions of the categories of professionals derive from each state's law and, therefore, vary from state to state. In some instances, two (or more) states will use the same term to describe a different group of professionals; in other instances, identical categories of professionals will be described by different terms.

To accommodate the disparity in terminology, you must either (1) determine the correct term for your professionals by reference to each state's law and customize each URS submission accordingly or (2) provide generic information on the URS from which each state can readily make the necessary determinations under its law.

You may comply with Item 20's requirements by choosing option (1), above, but the item is structured to implement option (2). The two examples that follow illustrate complete option (2) replies:

(a) "Great Telemarketing, Inc., 543 First Ave, New York, NY, 10036, 212-555-1212; plans and manages telephone campaign for public support and awareness; GTI charges us $4.50 per completed call plus $1.50 per pledge; our contract with GTI is from January 1, 1999 to December 31, 1999; the campaign will run from April 1999 through October 1999; GTI, through another firm it employs, solicits donations on our behalf; GTI does not itself handle donations but employs the caging company that receives, logs and deposits contributions."

(b) "John James & Associates, 325 Mason St, San Francisco, CA 94111, 415-989-8765; designs and manages direct mail campaigns for recruiting and retaining members; we pay JJA a fee of $1000 per month plus $45 per thousand letters mailed; our contract with JJA runs from July 1, 1998 through June 30, 1999; the campaign is continuous; JJA does not solicit contributions; JJA does not have custody or control of contributions, replies come directly to our P.O. box."

[There is no specified format for responding to Item 20. However, especially if you are reporting multiple professionals, organizing the required information in a chart or table may help assure that your response is complete and clear.]

Finally, and **VERY IMPORTANT,** you *must* provide accurate information as to whether or not the listed professionals are engaged in fundraising in each state in which you are filing the URS. You may address this issue by listing the respective states with each firm entry (e.g., to the GTI entry above, you might add: "only conducts campaigns for us in New York, New Jersey, Ohio, Illinois and Pennsylvania."). But regardless of method, *absent a clear indication to the contrary, each state receiving the URS will assume that all firms listed are subject to its law* and will proceed accordingly with enforcement.

**NOTE:** Some states require that you *submit copies of all your contracts* with retained outside fundraising professionals. See the state-by-state Appendix.

Item #21: List the total amount paid in fees and attributable expenses to any outside fundraising professionals during the previous reporting year. Specify the period covered by this total (e.g., "fiscal year running from July 1, 1997 through June 30, 1998"). Most or all of this total should derive from **line 30(a) of the IRS 990.**

Item #22: (A) List total contributions for previous reporting year. Specify time period. The item 22A total should be the same number that appears on **line 1d of the IRS 990** (or on line 1 of the 990EZ).

(B) List total fundraising costs for previous year. Specify time period. The item 22B total should be the same number that appears on **line 15 of the IRS 990** (there is no equivalent on the 990EZ).

(C) List total management & general costs for previous year. Specify time period. The item 22C total should be the same number that appears on **line 14 of the IRS 990** (No 990EZ equivalent).

(D) Express the ratio of fundraising costs to funds raised as a percentage (divide 22B by 22A).

(E) Express the ratio of fundraising costs plus management & general costs to funds raised as a percentage (divide 22B+22C by 22A).

Signature Box: **Signatures may not be photocopied.** Each submitted copy of the URS must be executed with *original signatures*. Requirements vary as to who must sign (i.e., which official of the nonprofit) and whether the signatures must be notarized. Refer to the state-by-state Appendix to *assure that the designated official(s) has signed* for the respective state and that the signature(s) has been *notarized, if required.* A few states stipulate that signers are making certain specific representations by signing and submitting the URS. This information can be found in the "required signatures" entry in the Appendix.

## A few REMINDERS:

1. Before submitting a URS to any state, *make sure you have checked the state-by-state Appendix* for all items that must accompany the URS.

2. Renewal registrants *need not re-submit* governance documents unless they have been amended (see 5, below).

3. Please *do not leave any URS items blank.* Entering "N/A" (not applicable), or some other appropriate message, will assure the reviewing official that you have not inadvertently omitted a required reply.

4. The URS is to be used for *registration filings* (initial or renewal). Ordinarily, it **can not be used for annual financial reporting.** Annual financial reporting is a parallel, but separate and distinct from registration, filing requirement under most state solicitation laws (see page 1 of Introduction to URS, "What is 'Registration'?").

5. Registrants in all states assume a *continuous obligation to keep their registrations accurate and up to date*. So, for example, in a state with one-time registration, a registrant is required to forward changes in governing documents, a task that would otherwise be accomplished with registration renewal. Similarly, in states requiring copies of fundraising contracts as part of registration, new or amended contracts entered into *after* registration (or *during* the registration period, in renewal states) must be filed immediately upon execution (since a filed contract is a prerequisite to solicitation in many jurisdictions).

6. **All filers** of the URS should *check the website* (http://www.nonprofits.org/library/gov/urs/) for updates to this packet. **Continual changes will be made** to *this* version of the URS packet (though no changes at all were made to ver. 1.0 during its 18-month life) as the need arises. In effect, the Web version of the URS packet will always be the "official," up-do-date version. Visitors to the site will find the most recent packet *and* they will be directed to information that itemizes, cumulatively, all changes introduced to the ver. 2.00 packet.

So that filers and state officials may more readily identify the documents they are working with, we have developed the following protocol for reflecting changes to the original 2.00 document:

- Minor (but material) changes to instructions, filing information, etc. (such as mailing address, fees, and the like) will be indicated by successive changes to the last digit in the version number. So, for example, the first batch of minor changes will be introduced into ver. 2.01 (and so on, to 2.02, 2.03, etc.).
- Significant changes (such as the addition of new states, the elimination of a supplement, etc.) will be indicated by successive changes to the first digit after the decimal. So, for example, when Wisconsin agrees to accept the URS and its information gets included in the Appendix, the changes will be introduced into ver. 2.10.

**Filers and state officials please note:** Only a material change to the URS form itself (such as the addition or elimination of existing questions), will produce a change in the first digit of the version number (e.g., to ver. 3.00). Therefore, absent intervening circumstances such as statutory changes (which would be posted on the website as soon as we have the information), all states currently accepting ver. 2.00 will also accept successive URS versions that begin with the number two (2.xx).

\*

# FUND-RAISING ISSUES

**Part I—Car Donation Programs**
**by Ray Seeley, Michael Seto, Debra Kawecki and Dave Jones**

> "We know that there are people that donate cars that have no wheels, no glass, the hood's gone, the transmission's in the trunk, and there's grass growing out of the floorboards."

> Steve Spriggs, director of development for the Sierra Vista Children's Center; quoted from the September 28, 1998, issue of the Chronicle of Philanthropy

The purpose of this article is to alert Exempt Organizations Tax Law Specialists about certain practices that occur in some car donation programs. The National Office views this as a growing area of noncompliance.

It is now common to turn on your radio, television or the internet and be exposed to an advertisement encouraging you to donate your car to charity. Many of these advertisements are from charities that receive cars so that they can use them in a sheltered workshop, refurbish them to give to the needy and other direct uses of the automobiles in the organization's charitable program. Some advertisements are from small organizations who receive a few cars that they resell themselves. This article does not concern those organizations.

The focus of this article is on organizations who have permitted third party entrepreneurs to use their names to solicit contributions of cars; to plan and to place advertising for donations; to take delivery on the cars (or pick them up if they are not in running condition); to complete the legal paper work; and to sell them typically at auction or to junk yards or to scrap dealers.

Some small percentage of the amount recovered or a flat fee may be provided to the charity that lent its name to this program. Often charities perform no oversight in the process, leaving it up to the third party entrepreneurs to operate the program as they see fit. Perhaps because the charities have no control over the advertising practices of the third party they are dealing with, many claims we see are more outrageous than the ones that preceded it. If there is a common characteristic of these programs, it is that many charities have abdicated responsibility for the things that are done in their names.

This article refers to these practices as "suspect vehicle donation plans or programs" in order to distinguish them from the programs run by organizations that use the vehicles directly in their charitable programs or take an active role in the donation process. A typical advertisement for a suspect vehicle donation plan contains the following statements.

> Turn Your Junk Into Jewels
> Let ABC EO turn your old car into cash for you.
> Take full BLUE BOOK Value!!!!!!

## 1. The Problems

There are potential negative tax consequences both for the donor and for the exempt organizations participating in suspect vehicle donation programs. While this article refers to charities, it applies to any exempt organization that can receive deductible contributions.

The difficulty for the donor is obvious. Most donors, relying on the representations in the advertising, assume that the donations are deductible under IRC 170. But are they? If they are, how much is deductible? The standard books available for evaluating the worth of a car, the "Blue Books", are based on the condition of the car. Most, if not all of the methods presume that the car is running and then evaluate it according to its condition, mileage, etc.

Many of the car donation advertisements claim that the donor can deduct full Blue Book value. It is well settled law that a deduction cannot exceed the fair market value of the item donated. The donor may not be entitled to a deduction or, if he is entitled to a deduction, the deduction may be overstated if the vehicle is not in running order.

The problems for the charity may be even greater. In a handful of situations, promoters may be using the program to enrich themselves. This article discusses issues of private benefit, inurement, substantial nonexempt purposes and the possible involvement of IRC 4958.

In order for this arrangement to meet requirements of IRC 170, the charity will most likely have to provide the substantiation statements required under IRC 170(f)(8); and to acknowledge that qualified written appraisals relating to the vehicles if donations worth more than $5000 are made. The donor must produce both the statement and the acknowledgment (if necessary) to substantiate a claimed contribution. Whether it does the paperwork itself, or whether the paperwork is done on its behalf; the charity must ensure that this paperwork is done accurately because there are penalties for aiding and abetting in the preparation of a false return.

There is a question of how to characterize the income received by the charity. If the charity receives a payment from a third party, the donated goods exception of IRC 513(a)(3) will not be available. The exclusion of royalty payments from unrelated business income rules exception may be available in some cases. However, where contributions are not deductible, an exempt organization may not be able to make a claim that the income is exclusively a royalty payment if it flows from the sale of a right which the taxpayer cannot license— the right to receive deductible contributions.

The Service is not alone in its concern about abuses in this area. California, for example, is in the forefront in having recently enacted legislation in an attempt to curtail the abuse of inflated appraisals. The September 28, 1998, issue of the Chronicle of Philanthropy, describes the passage of the new law.

> Gov. Pete Wilson of California has approved a measure passed by the Legislature that is intended to crack down on donors who take excessive charitable tax deductions for gifts of used cars, boats, and airplanes.
>
> The new law requires a charity—or a "commercial fund raiser" working for a charity—to provide a receipt to the donor within 90 days of the date the gift was made that describes the condition of the gift. If the charity sells the vehicle to a dismantler before it issues the receipt, it has to include in the receipt the amount the dismantler paid for the vehicle.

## 2. Typical Relationships

At the heart of the problems just discussed in suspect car donation cases, is the relationship between the charities and the for-profit entrepreneurs. The relationships are generally determined by contract. The legal status of the parties is often a useful key to their tax status. The relationships vary widely— program to program. Possible relationships are: agent and principal; joint venturers; licensor and licensee; and employer and independent contractor hired to perform a service.

These issues are made even more complex because certain terms may have different meanings under state law. For example, titling and its exact meaning may vary from state to state.

## 3. Deductibility

To be deductible, a contribution must be "to" or "for the use of" an organization described in IRC 170(c). Whether a contribution is "to" an organization is based on whether the donee organization has full control of the donation and discretion as to its use. See Rev. Rul. 62-113, 1962-2 C.B. 10.

The following fact pattern is typical in many suspect vehicle donation plans. Example I - A is an IRC 501(c)(3) organization. A has entered into a contract with professional fund-raiser Z. The fund-raising is to take place in the State of M. M's titling laws require owners' to appear in the chain of title. Owners cannot appoint agents to hold title for them.

The contract contains the following terms: 1. Z is given the right to advertise and solicit donations of motor vehicles and to give "tax deductible receipts" in the name of "A" to the donors of the items; 2. Z will receive and keep proceeds from the sales of the donated items.; 3. Z pays all of the costs related to the solicitation and sales of the donated items.; 4. Z will hold A harmless from any liability of any kind.; 5. A is not responsible for any facet of the project except to provide endorsement when requested.; 6. Z is appointed A's agent to sign all documents and handle matters relating to dealer's licensing.; 7. As full consideration for the rights under this contract Z pays A a fixed amount of $4,000 per month.

Both A and Z hold M Class 'B' Used Vehicle Dealer licenses. In operating the program, the donor assigns the vehicle's title to the charity. Z, in its capacity of A's agent, reassigns it to itself. A never takes possession of the vehicle.

In this fact pattern, A has neither control over the donated vehicles, nor discretion as to their use. Under the contract, A is not involved in reviewing the advertising or exercising any discretion as to the solicitations. Once Z takes possession, A plays no role in any decision as to their use.

The titling process, while nominally designed to incorporate A in the chain of title in order to satisfy the legal requirements of M is insufficient to show agency. A does not take possession of a vehicle or even oversee that aspect of the transaction. In fact, A has abdicated any oversight in titling them.

Another factor, weighing against the idea that these vehicles have been donated to A, is the way A is compensated under the contract. A, or an employee or agent of A properly delegated, could have conducted the program. In the agency situation, A would normally bear the risk of loss. While this one factor may not by itself be determinative, it combined with the others indicate that donations of the vehicles hasn't been made to A.

A exercises no discretion as to the vehicles' disposition. It makes no decisions over whether they are sold as used cars or sold at auction. It is difficult to see that disposition isn't an important part of their use.

These facts, when read together indicate that A does not exercise the kind of control and discretion required by Rev. Rul. 62-113.

"For the use of" generally refers to donations made in trust or similar arrangement. Davis v. United States, 495 U.S. 472, 481 (1990). Under the situation discussed in the example, the donations are not made in trust or similar arrangement so they cannot be "for the use of" A.

## 4. Private Benefit in General

Reg 1.501(c)(3)-1(c) provides that an organization will be regarded as operated exclusively for one or more exempt purposes only if it engages primarily in activities which accomplish one or more of such exempt purposes specified in section 501(c)(3). An organization will not be so regarded if more than an insubstantial part of its activities is not in furtherance of an exempt purpose. (emphasis added).

Reg. 1.501(c)(3)-1(d)(1)(ii) provides that an organization is not organized or operated exclusively for charitable purposes unless it serves a public rather than a private interest. Accordingly, the regulations provide,

> it is necessary for an organization to establish that it is not organized or operated for the benefit of private interests such as designated individuals, the creator or his family, shareholders of the organization, or persons controlled, directly or indirectly, by such private interests.

If an organization serves a public interest and also serves a private interest other than incidentally, it is not entitled to exemption under section 501(c)(3). This proposition is simply an expression of the basic principle underlying the enforcement of charitable trusts and exemption from federal income taxation under section 501(c)(3).

It is a settled principle of charity law that a charity's property is devoted to purposes which are considered beneficial to the community in general, rather than particular individuals. See, IV A. Scott on Trusts, Sec. 348 (3d ed. 1967).

Thus, although an organization's operations may be deemed to be beneficial to the public, if it also serves private interests other than incidentally, it is not entitled to exemption.

The word "incidental" in this context has both qualitative and quantitative meanings. To be incidental in a qualitative sense the benefit to the public cannot be achieved without necessarily benefitting certain private individuals. An example of this qualitative aspect is provided by Rev. Rul. 70-186, 1970-1 C.B. 128.

In Rev. Rul. 70-186 an organization was formed to preserve a lake as a public recreational facility and to improve the condition of the water in the lake to enhance its recreational features. Although the organization clearly benefitted the public, there necessarily was also significant benefit to the private individuals who owned lake front property. It was determined that the private benefit was incidental in a qualitative sense. Any private benefit derived by the lake front property owners did not lessen the public benefit flowing from the organization's operations. In fact, it would have been impossible for the organization to accomplish its purposes without providing benefits to the lake front property owners.

There is also a quantitative meaning to the term "incidental" private benefit. If the organization's activity provides a substantial benefit to private interests, even indirectly, it will negate charitability and exemption under IRC 501(c)(3). The substantiality of the private benefit is measured in the context of the overall public benefit conferred by the activity.

In Rev. Rul. 76-152, 1976-1 C.B. 151, a group of art patrons formed an organization to promote community understanding of modern art trends. The organization selected modern art works of local artists for exhibit at its gallery, which was open to the public. If an art work was sold, the gallery retained a commission of ten percent and paid the remainder to the artist. Direct economic benefit was conferred on the individual artists by the gallery's sale and rental of the art works that defeated exemption even though the organization's other activities furthered the arts.

## 5. Captive Programs

Present in vehicle donation programs, as in some other fund-raising situations is the possibility that promoters can take advantage of the format, solicit vehicles publicly, do little or no charity with the primary object of enriching themselves. This raises the question of whether the organization is operated for a private benefit in both a qualitative and a quantitative sense.

Consider the following example of a captive program. Example 2: Y is an automobile dealer in the state of M who is familiar with the automobile business. He sees the car donation programs as a way to make additional revenue. To this end, he creates charity B. Charity B applies for and receives recognition of exemption under IRC 501(c)(3). In its application for recognition, it represents that is going to be involved in educating the public on health issues.

After recognition Y enters into a contract with B, which he controls, similar to the contract in Example 1. One major difference, however, is a provision that hires Y as B's "agent" to run one aspect of its overall charitable program. Under the arrangement Y will set up a web page that has links to the national disease prevention programs. The bulk of the web page is devoted to soliciting vehicle donations. Potential donors are offered significant premiums for participating in the program. These include discount books and tickets in new car raffles.

Needless to say, this prize structure greatly increases the cost of the program and reduces the amount that B receives. While B retains a small percentage of the gross (as opposed to a flat fee) at the end of each month, it has yet to devote the proceeds to any charitable endeavor.

The true beneficiary of this suspect vehicle donation program seems to be Y, the automobile dealer. He arranges the transaction, takes delivery on or picks up the vehicles, resells the vehicles or cannibalizes them for their parts, and turns over a prearranged percentage to the charity. None of this could happen without the charity. If the charity did not participate and lend its tax exempt status to the transactions, there would be no trading in donated cars. If B does nothing with the proceeds during the years under examination, can one argue that B is not operated for private benefit during those years in a qualitative sense? Is it operated to serve a private benefit in a quantitative sense?

Inurement, a particular form of private benefit is discussed in the next session. The distinct characteristic of inurement is that it involves an inappropriate diversion of funds.

## 6. Inurement

To meet the operational test, an organization must not be operated for the benefit of designated individuals or the persons who created it. Regs. 1.501(c)(3)-1(d)(1)(ii). An organization's trustees, officers, members, founders, or contributors may not, by reason of their position, acquire any of its funds. If funds are diverted from exempt purposes to private purposes exemption is in jeopardy.

The Code specifically forbids the inurement of earnings to the benefit of insiders, private shareholders or individuals. Further, the regulations state that an organization is not operated exclusively for the statutory purposes if its net earnings inure to the benefit of individuals. Regs. 1.501(c)(3)-1(c)(2).

The prohibition of inurement, in its simplest terms, means that a private share-holder or individual cannot misappropriate the organization's funds to himself except as reasonable payment for goods or services.

Deferred or retained interests in the organization's assets may be a form of indirect benefit not permitted by the statute. Where the officers of a school leased property to the school and caused it to erect expensive improvements which would benefit them individually when the lease expired, exemption was denied. Texas Trade School, 30 T.C. 642 (1968), aff'd 272 F.2d 168 (5th Cir. 1959). In the suspect vehicle program, if the broker is an insider and causes the organization to enter into a transaction that is economically detrimental to the exempt organization and good for the insider, inurement issues arise.

In Rev. Rul. 66-259, 1966-2 C.B. 214, the creator of a charitable trust retained a reversionary interest in trust assets, and exemption was denied. Under the terms of the trust agreement, any increase in the value of the trust assets would become part of principal and would return to the creator at the time he took possession of his reversionary interest. Similarly, with the suspect vehicle donation program the donor and broker receive the lion's share of the benefits while the charity is providing the acknowledgment that makes the deal possible.

IRC 501(c)(3) does not prohibit all dealings between a charitable organization and its founder or with those in controlling positions. However, where individuals controlling the organization receive funds that rightfully belong to the organization, exemption is precluded because of inurement. Suppose, for example, Y, in example 2, understated the income to the program, this would reduce B's income and because Y is an insider, constitute inurement.

## 7.  IRC 4958

Section 4958 was added to the Code by the Taxpayer Bill of Rights 2, P.L. 1044-168. It generally applies to excess benefit transactions occurring on or after September 14, 1995.

An excess benefit transaction (EBT) is any transaction in which an economic benefit provided by an applicable tax-exempt organization to, or for the use of, any disqualified person exceeds the value of consideration received by the organization in exchange for the benefit. A disqualified person is any person who was, at any time during the 5-year period ending on the date of the excess benefit transaction, in a position to exercise substantial influence over the affairs of the organization.

There are three taxes under IRC 4958. Disqualified persons are liable for the first two taxes, under IRC 4958(a)(1), a tax of 25 percent of the excess benefit must be paid by any disqualified person who benefits from an EBT. Under IRC 4958(b), a tax of 200 percent must be paid by any disqualified person who benefits from an EBT if the transaction is not corrected. Under IRC 4958(a)(2) a tax of 10 percent of the excess benefit must be paid by any organization manager who participates in an EBT knowingly, willfully, and without reasonable cause.

Does IRC 4958 tax apply to example 2?

## 8. Unrelated Business Income Tax

IRC 512(b)(2) excludes from unrelated business taxable income:

> [A] all royalties (including overriding royalties) whether measured by production or by gross or taxable income from the property, and all deductions directly connected with that income.

The term "royalties" is not defined in either the Internal Revenue Code or the regulations. Reg. 1.512(b)-1 provides that whether a particular item of income falls within any of the modifications provided in IRC 512(b) (which includes "royalties") shall be determined by all the facts and circumstances of each case.

The issue of whether income under certain types of arrangements constitutes a "royalty" has been the subject of revenue rulings and numerous court decisions.

Rev. Rul. 81-178, 1981-2 C.B. 135, holds that payments an exempt labor organization receives from various business enterprises for the use of the organization's trademark and similar properties are royalties within the meaning of section 512(b)(2) of the Code and are not taken into account in determining unrelated taxable income. However, payments the organization receives for personal appearances and interviews by its members are not royalties but are compensation for personal services and must be taken into account in computing the organization's unrelated business taxable income.

> To be a royalty, a payment must relate to the use of a valuable right. Payments for the use of trademarks, trade names, service marks, or copyrights, whether or not payment is based on the use made of such property, are ordinarily classified as royalties for federal tax purposes.

The ruling also noted that, although excluded from UBIT as a royalty, the income from the licensing activity was income from unrelated trade or business since the licensing agreements did not directly promote the group's exempt purposes.

There are many different forms the arrangement between the exempt organization and the promoter can take. For purposes of this discussion, we are only considering the arrangement where by the exempt organization permits the third party broker to use its name in marketing its donation program. In return, the exempt organization receives a fee which is calculated as a percentage of gross receipts.

If this was the entire agreement, royalty treatment might be appropriate. But that is not all that is happening here. Promoters are typically given the right to claim that contributors to the program can take deductions for their donations. The fact that contributions other than to the charities or their agents are not deductible raises questions as to whether the income is a royalty. Second, by providing the substantiation required by IRC 170(f)(8) and acknowledging appraisals of donations worth more than $5000, the organization is providing services that may preclude royalty treatment as well. See Rev. Rul. 81-178, 1981-2 C.B. 135.

## 9. Penalties

Under the Tax Equity and Fiscal Responsibility Act of 1982, Congress enacted IRC 6700 and IRC 6701 as penalties for the abuse of tax shelters. IRC 6700 imposes a penalty on anyone—promoters, salesmen and their assistants— for organizing and selling abusive tax shelters. IRC 6701 is the aiding and abetting provision, and it imposes a penalty on those who aid and assist in the preparation of false or fraudulent tax documents that would result in an understatement of tax liability. (See 1999 CPE, Topic M, Application of IRC 6700 and IRC 6701 To Charitable Contribution Deductions, p. 261, for further discussion).

These two provisions could be applicable in the exempt organizations area. Charities often receive gifts of property from contributors either as a fundraiser or so that they may carry out their charitable endeavors. IRC 170(c) provides that such contributions are tax deductible for federal income tax purposes provided that certain requirements are met. One requirement, under IRC 170(f)(8)(A), is that a contribution of $250 or more, whether in cash or property, is tax deductible only if that contributor has a contemporaneous written acknowledgment from the donee organization. (See 1997 CPE, Topic G, Updates on Disclosure and Substantiation Rules, p. 67, for further discussion of this provision.)

Another is contained in Reg. 1.170A-13(c). This regulation requires that contributors of property worth more than $5000 receive "qualified written appraisals." The donee organization must sign the appraisal summary. In this situation, the charity is not attesting the validity or accuracy of the appraisal, but is acknowledging that it has received the donated property.

Failure to satisfy these provisions can lead to the loss of the tax deduction.

The current working supposition is that these two requirements interplay with IRC 6701 in the vehicle donation situation, where no deductible contribution is appropriate. There a charity's attempted delegation of its paperwork obligations under IRC 170(f)(8) and with respect to qualified written appraisals result in documents that individuals can use to understate income tax liability. The only factual question is whether a charity "knows (or has reason to believe (IRC 6701(a)(2)) that its actions result in an understatement.

The same reasoning applies where a charity has not delegated its obligations. In other words, where a charity itself prepares the IRC 170 substantiation statements and signs the qualified written appraisal summaries, it also may be involved in aiding and abetting the understatement of tax liability if no deduction is appropriate.

Even where a contribution is appropriate, failure to properly supervise excessive claims concerning deductibility (e.g., cars without motors can result in deductions equal to blue book value) may result in an overstatement of a tax deduction under IRC 6701 (or so it would seem if a principal is responsible for the actions of his agent under IRC 6781).

Topic M of the 1999 CPE article referred to earlier discusses the IRC 6700 penalty and its application to the third party entrepreneurs who actually run the suspect programs.

## 10. Service Response

On May 27, 1999, the Director, Exempt Organizations Technical Division (OP:E:EO) issued a memorandum to the Regional Chief Compliance Officers entitled Used Car Donation Programs. The memorandum discusses the issue and contains the following alert.

We are concerned that some of this advertising is misleading or, in some instances, false, and is being used inappropriately. Key districts should be alert to the advertising that is being conducted in their districts and should consider conducting examinations if the facts warrant. Key district should consider using the tax shelter penalties in appropriate cases. It is possible that some abusive contractual arrangements may result is excessive private benefit and thus jeopardize the exempt status of the charities involved . . . In appropriate cases, referrals of individual donors to the examination function should be considered.

## Part II - Scrip Programs
## by Michael Seto and Dave Jones

### 1. Introduction

Many charities conduct fund-raising activities that offer benefits to their patrons in return for contributions. Traditional activities of this type include bake sales and golf tournaments. One such effort to increase revenue involves participation in "scrip" programs.

### 2. "Scrip" Programs

A "scrip" program is a fundraiser whereby merchants issue gift certificates at a discount to charities through a "scrip operator." The scrip have face values and can be used to purchase goods or services. The scrip operator administers the scrip program and negotiates with each participating merchant to set the prices that the charities will pay for the scrip. It arranges for the distribution of the scrip to participating charities. It also provides support services for the scrip program, such as telephone operators, toll-free phone and fax, order processing, inventory fulfillment, shipping, tracking, and computerized database accounting systems.

The purchase price that a charity pays for the scrip is a certain percentage (usually ten percent) below the face value of the scrip. The difference between the discounted purchase price and the face value of the scrip represents a charity's proceeds from the fund-raising program. The charity sells the scrip at face value to its members. The scrip operator would receive from the merchants a percentage (one percent, for example) of the face value of the scrip that is sold by the charity.

### 3. Charitable Contribution or Purchase Price?

IRC 170(c) allows deductions for charitable contributions. The basic rules of whether a payment is made as a gift or as a purchase price for the purchase of goods or services is discussed in Rev. Rul. 67-246, 1967-2 C.B. 104. To qualify as a charitable contribution, a payment to a charity must be a gift with no expectation of receiving a benefit in return. Where a payment is made in return for an item or benefit, the presumption is that such payment is the purchase price and not a gift. The payment represents the fair market value of the item or benefit and, therefore, is not tax deductible. To rebut the presumption, the taxpayer must show that:

- the payment made for the item or benefit exceeds the fair market value of that item or benefit; and
- the excess payment is made with the intent to make a gift.

The first requirement is satisfied by evidence that the payment exceeds the fair market value of the item or benefit received. The second requirement is satisfied if the surrounding facts and circumstances of the payment indicate the taxpayer's knowledge that the payment exceeded fair market value and the intent that it be a gift.

In the scrip program, a taxpayer makes a payment to a charity in return for scrip. The presumption is that the payment made for the scrip is the purchase price. Unless it can be shown that (a) the payment made for the scrip exceeds its fair market value; and (b) the excess payment is made with the intent to make a gift, the payment cannot be considered a gift.

## A. Example 1

Charity A purchased one thousand scrip booklets through Y, the scrip organizer, at a ten percent discount from face value. Each booklet has a face value of $100 and contains ten pieces of scrip, each with a denomination of $10. Each scrip is redeemable for goods purchased at X, a store. John Doe purchased a scrip booklet from Charity A for $100. Since the payment equals the market value of the booklet when redeemed at X, the $100 is the purchase price of the scrip and not a gift. John Doe may not deduct any part of the payment to Charity A as a charitable contribution.

## B. Example 2

The facts are the same as above except for the following. Charity A sets the sale price of each booklet at $225. John Doe purchases a booklet from Charity A for $225, knowing that its fair market value is $100 and intending the $125 excess payment to be a gift. At the time of the sale to John Doe, Charity A provides him with a letter that contains the following information: a good faith estimate of the $100 fair market value of the scrip booklet provided in exchange for the $225 (in this case the estimate was simple because the booklet was worth $100 of goods or services); and stating that the amount of the payment that is tax deductible for federal tax purposes is the difference between the fair market value of the scrip booklet and John Doe's payment. Since the payment exceeds the fair market value of the booklet and that excess is intended as a gift, John Doe may claim a charitable contribution of $125.

## 4. Quid Pro Quo Contributions

The situation described in Example 2 is a "quid pro quo contribution". It is a payment made partly as a contribution and partly as a payment for goods or services. In 1993, legislation was enacted that required charities to advise individuals of the rules relating to "quid-pro-quo" gifts when they were involved in fund-raising programs that feature them. (See IRC 6115(b).) See in the 1997 CPE, Topic G, Updates on Disclosure and Substantiation Rules, at pp. 67-81, for a detailed discussion. For the first time charities were required, in IRC 6115, to inform donors about the requirements of IRC 170 if the charities engage in fund-raising programs using "quid-pro-quo" gifts.

IRC 6115 provides that if a quid-pro-quo contribution involves a payment of more than $75, charities must provide to the contributor in connection with the solicitation a receipt of the contribution and a written disclosure statement that contains the following information:

- A good-faith estimate of the fair market value of the goods or services provided in return for the contribution;
- A statement that the amount of the contribution the donor may deduct for Federal income tax purposes is reduced by the fair market value of the goods or services received in return for the contribution.

In example 2 above, Charity A conformed with the requirements of IRC 6115.

IRC 6714(a) provides that a penalty of $10 per contribution is imposed on organizations that do not meet the disclosure requirement of IRC 6115. This provision also provides that the maximum penalty for a fund-raising event or mailing is $5,000.

## 5. Donor Substantiation Requirements

In 1993, Congress enacted a second piece of legislation that has some bearing on scrip programs. IRC 170(f)(8)(A) provides that no deduction is allowed under IRC 170 for a contribution of $250 or more in cash or property unless the taxpayer has a contemporaneous written statement from the charity substantiating the donation. IRC 170(f)(8) has less of an impact on scrip programs than IRC 6115 because most scrip programs involve sales of less than $250. For a detailed discussion of substantiation rules in general, se the 1997 CPE article, Topic G.

In example 2 above, Charity A's letter to John Doe contain sufficient information to satisfy the substantiation requirements of IRC 170(f)(8). Although Mr. Doe is not required to have a written letter from Charity A for IRC 170(f)(8) purposes because the contribution was less than $250, Charity A is required to make a disclosure under IRC 6115 because Mr. Doe's payment was a quid pro quo contribution and the amount was more than $75. Where no gift is involved, as was the case in example 1, no substantiation statement is required.

The penalty for failure to obtain the substantiation statement required by IRC 170(f)(8) falls, in the first instance, on the contributor. Although charities are involved in issuing the statement, Congress does not impose on charities a penalty for failure to furnish an IRC 170(f)(8) statement. The belief was that where donors of $250 or more could not take a deduction because they were not given properly completed substantiation statements, the donors would punish the charity by not giving to them in the future. Charities on the other hand would see substantiation as an element in good donor relations. A charity that knowingly provided false written substantiation to a donor might be subject to the penalties for aiding and abetting an understatement of tax liability under IRC 6701.

## 6. The For-Profit Provider

As indicated earlier, for-profit scrip providers are integrally involved in many of the scrip programs. Although the operators are actively involved in promoting the business, they are not, unlike the car donation promoters discussed earlier, selling scrip to donor/consumers. In scrip programs, the selling/soliciting donation process is done at the grass-roots levels by the charities. Typically they are non-profit schools, local arts organizations, youth organizations, and churches. IRC 6115 and to a lesser extent IRC 170(f)(8) are the primary compliance tools available.

In addition to the above material, other portions of the IRS CPE text address fund-raising law issues. Most notably is Topic I, which concerns use of the Internet in fund-raising and similar activities. A summary of this material follows.

There are many salient statements in the CPE text but none more so than this: "[T]he use of the Internet to accomplish a particular task does not change the way the tax laws apply to that task. Advertising is still advertising and fundraising is still fundraising." Still, there are those who think that an activity engaged in by means of the Internet is somehow different for tax law purposes.

The text includes reminders as to charitable gifts of money. (Noncash gifts are not discussed because they generally are not made directly over the Internet.) It is still necessary to be certain tht the recipient of the contribution is a charity. If the donee is a charity, the gift may not be earmarked for a specific individual or for an organization that is not entitled to receive charitable contributions.

Again, the substantiation requirements (§ 6.2) apply, as do the rules as to quid pro quo contributions (§ 6.4) and appraisals. The disclosure rules for noncharitable contributions (§ 6.5) are also applicable to solicitations over the Internet.

There is a brief discussion in the CPE text of solicitation of charitable contributions by means of a charity's web page. As the text points out, this activity does not raise any "novel tax issues." (Again, as noted, donors need to be certain that the gifts are to qualifying organizations and for qualified purposes.) Then, however, there is a marvelous understatement: "For the charities themselves, a greater concern may be the applicability of state and local laws requiring registration before soliciting contributions. There is some concern that states and local governments will argue that if any resident of their jurisdiction can access a website and thus see a solicitation, the charity must register." No jurisdiction has yet adopted that stance (§ 8.15B) but think of the time and financial burdens were that to happen!

The text discusses "third-party sites." These are for-profit companies that post a list of charitable organizations. The mission statements are provided, along with a link to charities' own web sites if they have one. Gifts are made by credit card. Some time may pass (such as a month) before the company remits the net gifts to the charities. The company retains a portion of the gift (such as 15 percent) as an administrative fee.

Issues arise here, even assuming the donee is a bona fide charity. Is the third-party entity an agent of the charity? (The gift is first made to it.) Is this one of these situations where there is a deductible gift, even though the initial recipient is not a charity, since the funds are earmarked for a charity? The little law there is on the point suggests that, for deductibility to be available, the funds must be transferred to the charity frequently (e.g., weekly). A holding of the funds for a month may preclude deductibility. Moreover, are these third parties functioning a professional fund-raisers, requiring registration and reporting under some states' laws?

Regarding marketing, merchandising, advertising, and the like, the CPE text notes that the IRS "has yet to consider many of the questions raised" by these activities. (Considering the recent extent and growth of these activities, it is surprising that some guidance has not been forthcoming; as noted below, an announcement on the subject is in preparation.) Again, however, the text goes on to state that "it is reasonable to assume that as the Service position develops it will remain consistent with our position with respect to advertising and merchandising and publishing in the off-line world."

The text gingerly broaches the subject of charity website HyperText links to related or recommended sites. Link exchanges may be treated as mailing list exchanges. Compensation for a linkage may be unrelated business income. The purpose of the link may be determinative: is its purpose furtherance of exempt purposes (a referral of the site visitor to additional (educational) information) or is it part of an unrelated activity (including advertising)?

Also involved are corporate sponsorships (§ 6.17), inasmuch as exempt organizations may seek corporate support to underwrite the production of all or a portion of the organization's website. These relationships may be short-term or continue on a long-term Basis. The financial support may be acknowledged by means of display of a corporate logo, notation of the sponsor's web address and/or 800 number, a "moving banner" (defined as a graphic advertisement, usually a moving image, measured in pixels), or a link. (The issue here is: is the support of a qualified sponsorship payment, in which case the revenue is not taxable, or is it advertising income, which generally is taxable as unrelated business income?).

The CPE text recognizes that there is a question as to whether the use of a link in an acknowledgment will change the character of a corporation's payment—convert it from corporate sponsorship to taxable advertising income. While not answering this question, the text seems to be sympathetic to the view that the payment should retain its character as a mere acknowledgment since the website visitor must take an "affirmative action" (if a click can be called that) to reach the corporation's website. A moving banner is more likely to be considered advertising.

Another problem relates to the rule that qualified sponsorship payments do not include payments that entitle the sponsors to acknowledgments to regularly scheduled printed material published by or on behalf of the tax-exempt organization. Here, the issue is the characterization of website materials. The IRS wrote: "Most of the materials made available on exempt organization websites are clearly prepared in a manner that is distinguishable from the methodology used in the preparation of periodicals."

Nonetheless, the IRS recognizes that there can be an online publication that is treated as a periodical. (When this is the case, the special rules by which unrelated business income from periodical advertising is computed become available.) Some periodicals have online editions and some print publications are reproduced on-line, sometimes on a subscription basis or in a members-only access portion of a website. The IRS observed that these "materials should be and generally are sufficiently segregated from the other traditional website materials so that the methodology employed in the production and distribution methods are clearly ascertainable and the periodical income and costs can be independently and appropriately determined." The text adds that presumably "genuine" periodicals has an editorial staff, marketing program, and budget independent of the organization's webmaster.

Then there is the matter of the "virtual trade show," which generates income for trade associations and other exempt entities from "virtual exhibitors." This brings into play the rules by which traditional trade show income is excluded from the unrelated business income tax (§ 6.6). The IRS wrote that the extent to which the traditional rules will apply to virtual trade show income "will most likely depend in large part on whether the qualifying organization [one described in IRC § 501(c)(3), (4), (5), or (6)] is able to demonstrate that its exhibits or displays are substantially similar to those traditionally carried on at a trade show."

The CPE text hints that the tax exclusion is not available for a mere listing of links to industry suppliers' websites. Also, it is "highly questionable" whether income from a year-round virtual trade show is excludable from unrelated business income. Conversely, virtual trade shows with displays including educational information related to issues of interest to industry members or those that are timed to coincide with the sponsoring organization's annual meeting or regular trade show may qualify for the exclusion.

Next: online storefronts, complete with virtual shopping carts, on exempt organization's websites. Again, the IRS expects to be using the same analysis that it applies in sales made through stores, catalogs, and other traditional vehicles. Reference was made to the treatment of museum gift shop sales (e.g., IRS Tech. Adv. Mem. 9720002). In deciding whether the unrelated business income tax applies, the IRS looks to the nature, scope, and motivation for the particular sales activities. Merchandise is evaluated on an item-by-item basis (applying the fragmentation rule) to determine whether the sales activity furthers the accomplishment of the organization's exempt purposes or is simply a way to increase revenue.

As to online auctions, the IRS is particularly concerned with charities' use of "outside auction service providers." The IRS recognized that utilization of these providers may provide a larger audience for the auction and enable the organization to avoid credit card problems but it cautions that the relationship "might have tax implications."

Again, the focus is on control. The IRS will consider how much control the charity exercises over the marketing and conduct of the auction. The IRS wants the charity to have "primary responsibility" in yhid trhstf. Otherwise, the IRS "may be more likely to view income from such auction activities as income from classified advertising rather than as income derived from the conduct of a fundraising event." A warning: the IRS stated that these service providers are "essentially professional fundraisers" (with implications as to state charitable solicitation acts), and thus their functions and fees should be scrutinized using the doctrines of private inurement and private benefit.

Finally, the IRS discussed affiliate and other co-venture programs with merchants. Of particular note was arrangements with large, online booksellers. Some exempt organizations make book recommendations that are displayed on their website; others have a link to the bookseller. The exempt organization earns a percentage of sales of recommended materials and perhaps also a commission on purchases sold through the referring link. The principal issue here is whether the resulting income is a tax-excludable royalty.

On this point, the IRS analogizes to the litigation involving the tax treatment mailing list and affinity card income. The IRS again stated its view that the marketing of a credit card by an exempt organization constitutes services typically provided by a commercial company. The CPE text also ruefully notes that this view has not prevailed in the many cases contested in the Tax Court.

This portion of the text concludes with a reference to the Treasury/IRS 1999 business plan, which contemplates the issuance of a request for comments on the application of the tax law to the Internet activities of exempt organizations. In addition to the unrelated business income issues, there are matters to be resolved in the realms of lobbying and political campaign intervention. Wrote the IRS: "It is hoped that all members of the exempt organizations [community] will be involved in the development of new policies which will build upon principles developed over time and adapt to allow exempt organizations to take advantage of the technological innovations of the new millennium."

# Table of Cases

p. 742, left column, line 34. *Replace "Murdoch" with "Murdock".*

# Supplement Table of Authorities

## Cases

*Alumni Ass'n of the University of Oregon, Inc.* v. *Commissioner* § 6.6(b)

*American Campaign Academy* v. *Commissioner,* §§ 6.15(b), 8.15C

*American Charities for Reasonable Fundraising Regulation, Inc.* v. *Pinellas County,* §§ 5.2, 5.3(c), 5.11

*American Target Advertising, Inc.* v. *Giani,* § 5.3

*Association of Charitable Games of Missouri* v. *Missouri Gaming Commission,* §§ 5.3(c), 5.5

*Camps Newfound/Owatonna, Inc.* v. *Town of Harrison, Maine,* § 5.2

*Church by Mail, Inc.* v. *Commissioner,* § 8.15C

*Common Cause* v. *Commissioner,* § 6.6(b)

*Connally* v. *General Construction Co.,* § 5.7A

*Dayton Area Visually Impaired Persons, Inc.* v. *Fisher,* § 5.3

*Disabled American Veterans* v. *Commissioner,* § 6.6(b)

*Disabled American Veterans* v. *United States,* § 6.6(b)

*Fernandes* v. *Limmer,* §§ 5.4, 5.11

*Fraternal Order of Police, Illinois State Troopers Lodge No. 41* v. *Commissioner,* § 6.6(b)

*Fund for the Study of Economic Growth & Tax Reform* v. *Internal Revenue Service,* § 8.15C

*Gospel Missions of America* v. *Bennett,* §§ 5.2, 5.3(c), 5.4, 5.6, 5.7(b), 5.7A, 5.11, 9.10

*Granzow* v. *Commissioner,* § 8.15C

*Holy Spirit Ass'n for Unification of World Christianity* v. *Hodge,* §§ 5.3(c), 5.11

*Hynes* v. *Mayor of Oradell,* §§ 5.6, 5.7A

*International Society for Krishna Consciousness of Houston, Inc.* v. *City of Houston,* § 5.3(c)

*KJ's Fund Raisers, Inc.* v. *Commissioner,* § 6.6

*Lakewood, City of* v. *Plain Dealer Publishing Co.,* § 5.6

*Mississippi State University Alumni, Inc.* v. *Commissioner,* § 6.6

*Murdock* v. *Pennsylvania,* § 5.11

*Nationalist Movement* v. *Commissioner,* § 8.15C

*Orange County Agricultural Society, Inc.* v. *Commissioner,* § 6.6(b)

*Oregon State University Alumni Ass'n, Inc.* v. *Commissioner,* § 6.6(b)

*Planned Parenthood Federation of America, Inc.* v. *Commissioner,* § 6.6(b)

*Sierra Club, Inc.* v. *Commissioner (Sierra Club I),* § 6.6(b)

*Sierra Club, Inc.* v. *Commissioner (Sierra Club II),* § 6.6(b)

*Sierra Club, Inc.* v. *Commissioner (Sierra Club III),* § 6.6(b)

# Cumulative Index

**Note:** Section numbers ending with "s" refer to sections in the supplement.

# INDEX